# SHAKESPEARE MADE EASY

**Modern version side-by-side with full original text**

# Romeo and Juliet

Edited and rendered into modern English by
Alan Durband

D1380373

## Hutchinson

London Melbourne Sydney Auckland Johannesburg

Hutchinson & Co. (Publishers) Ltd
An imprint of the Hutchinson Publishing Group
17–21 Conway Street, London W1P 6JD

Hutchinson Publishing Group (Australia) Pty Ltd
PO Box 496, 16–22 Church Street, Hawthorne,
Melbourne, Victoria 3122

Hutchinson Group (NZ) Ltd
32–34 View Road, PO Box 40–086, Glenfield, Auckland 10

Hutchinson Group (SA) (Pty) Ltd
PO Box 337, Bergvlei 2012, South Africa

First published 1984
© Alan Durband 1984

Photoset in Plantin and Univers by
Kelly Typesetting Limited, Bradford-on-Avon, Wiltshire

Printed and bound in Great Britain by
The Guernsey Press, Guernsey, Channel Islands

**British Library Cataloguing in Publication Data**

Shakespeare, William
   Romeo and Juliet.
   I. Title      II. Durband, Alan     III. Series
   822.3'3      PR2831

ISBN 0 09 155911 1

*'Reade him, therefore; and againe, and againe: And if then you do not like him, surely you are in some danger, not to understand him. . . .'*

John Hemming
Henry Condell

*Preface to the 1623 Folio Edition*

## Shakespeare Made Easy

Titles in the series

**Macbeth**
**The Merchant of Venice**
**Julius Caesar**
**Romeo and Juliet**

Other drama books edited by Alan Durband

# Contents

# Introduction

*Shakespeare Made Easy* is intended for readers approaching the plays for the first time, who find the language of Elizabethan poetic drama an initial obstacle to understanding and enjoyment. In the past, the only answer to the problem has been to grapple with the difficulties with the aid of explanatory footnotes (often missing when they are most needed) and a stern teacher. Generations of students have complained that 'Shakespeare was ruined for me at school'.

Usually a fuller appreciation of Shakespeare's plays comes in later life. Often the desire to read Shakespeare for pleasure and enrichment follows from a visit to the theatre, where excellence of acting and production can bring to life qualities which sometimes lie dormant on the printed page.

*Shakespeare Made Easy* can never be a substitute for the original plays. It cannot possibly convey the full meaning of Shakespeare's poetic expression, which is untranslatable. *Shakespeare Made Easy* concentrates on the dramatic aspect, enabling the novice to become familiar with the plot and characters, and to experience one facet of Shakespeare's genius. To know and understand the central issues of each play is a sound starting point for further exploration and development.

Discretion can be used in choosing the best method to employ. One way is to read the original Shakespeare first, ignoring the modern version – or using it only when interest or understanding flags. Another way is to read the translation first, to establish confidence and familiarity with plot and characters.

Either way, cross-reference can be illuminating. The modern text can explain 'what is being said' if Shakespeare's language is particularly complex or his expression antiquated. The Shakespeare text will show the reader of the modern paraphrase how much more can be expressed in poetry than in prose.

The use of *Shakespeare Made Easy* means that the newcomer need never be overcome by textual difficulties. From first to last, a measure of understanding is at hand – the key is provided for what has been a locked door to many students in the past. And as understanding grows, so an awareness develops of the potential of language as a vehicle for philosophic and moral expression, beauty, and the abidingly memorable.

Even professional Shakespearian scholars can never hope to arrive at a complete understanding of the plays. Each critic, researcher, actor or producer merely adds a little to the work that has already been done, or makes fresh interpretations of the texts for new generations. For everyone, Shakespearian appreciation is a journey. *Shakespeare Made Easy* is intended to help with the first steps.

# William Shakespeare

## His life

William Shakespeare was born in Stratford-on-Avon, Warwickshire, on 23 April 1564, the son of a prosperous wool and leather merchant. Very little is known of his early life. From parish records we know that he married Ann Hathaway in 1582, when he was eighteen, and she was twenty-six. They had three children, the eldest of whom died in childhood.

Between his marriage and the next thing we know about him, there is a gap of ten years. Probably he became a member of a travelling company of actors. By 1592 he had settled in London, and had earned a reputation as an actor and playwright.

Theatres were then in their infancy. The first (called *The Theatre*) was built in 1576. Two more followed as the taste for theatre grew: *The Curtain* in 1577 and *The Rose* in 1587. The demand for new plays naturally increased. Shakespeare probably earned a living adapting old plays and working in collaboration with others on new ones. Today we would call him a 'freelance', since he was not permanently attached to one theatre.

In 1594, a new company of actors, The Lord Chamberlain's Men was formed, and Shakespeare was one of the shareholders. He remained a member throughout his working life. The company regrouped in 1603, and was re-named The King's Men, with James I as their patron.

Shakespeare and his fellow-actors prospered. In 1598 they built their own theatre, *The Globe*, which broke away from the traditional rectangular shape of the inn and its yard (the early home of travelling bands of actors). Shakespeare described it in *Henry V* as 'this wooden O', because it was circular.

Many other theatres were built by investors eager to profit from the new enthusiasm for drama. *The Hope*, *The Fortune*,

*The Red Bull* and *The Swan* were all open-air 'public' theatres. There were also many 'private' (or indoor) theatres, one of which (*The Blackfriars*) was purchased by Shakespeare and his friends because the child actors who performed there were dangerous competitors. (Shakespeare denounces them in *Hamlet.*)

After writing some thirty-seven plays (the exact number is something which scholars argue about), Shakespeare retired to his native Stratford, wealthy and respected. He died on his birthday, in 1616.

## His plays

Shakespeare's plays were not all published in his lifetime. None of them comes to us exactly as he wrote it.

In Elizabethan times, plays were not regarded as either literature or good reading matter. They were written at speed (often by more than one writer), performed perhaps ten or twelve times, and then discarded. Fourteen of Shakespeare's plays were first printed in Quarto (17cm × 21cm) volumes, not all with his name as the author. Some were authorized (the 'good' Quartos) and probably were printed from prompt copies provided by the theatre. Others were pirated (the 'bad' Quartos) by booksellers who may have employed shorthand writers, or bought actors' copies after the run of the play had ended.

In 1623, seven years after Shakespeare's death, John Hemming and Henry Condell (fellow-actors and shareholders in The King's Men) published a collected edition of Shakespeare's works – thirty-six plays in all – in a Folio (21cm × 34cm) edition. From their introduction it would seem that they used Shakespeare's original manuscripts ('we have scarce received from him a blot in his papers') but the Folio volumes that still survive are not all exactly alike, nor are the plays printed as we know them today, with act and scene divisions and stage-directions.

A modern edition of a Shakespeare play is the result of a great deal of scholarly research and editorial skill over several centuries. The aim is always to publish a text (based on the good and bad Quartos and the Folio editions) that most closely resembles what Shakespeare intended. Misprints have added to the problems, so some words and lines are pure guesswork. This explains why some versions of Shakespeare's plays differ from others.

## His theatre

The first purpose-built playhouse in Elizabethan London, constructed in 1576, was *The Theatre*. Its co-founders were John Brayne, an investor, and James Burbage, a carpenter turned actor. Like the six or seven 'public' (or outdoor) theatres which followed it over the next thirty years, it was situated outside the city, to avoid conflict with the authorities. They disapproved of players and playgoing, partly on moral and political grounds, and partly because of the danger of spreading the plague. (There were two major epidemics during Shakespeare's lifetime, and on each occasion the theatres were closed for lengthy periods.)

*The Theatre* was a financial success, and Shakespeare's company performed there until 1598, when a dispute over the lease of the land forced Burbage to take down the building. It was re-created in Southwark, as *The Globe*, with Shakespeare and several of his fellow-actors as the principal shareholders.

By modern standards, *The Globe* was small. Externally, the octagonal building measured less than thirty metres across, but in spite of this it could accommodate an audience of between two and three thousand people. (The largest of the three theatres at the National Theatre complex in London today seats 1160.)

Performances were advertised by means of playbills posted around the city, and they took place during the hours of daylight when the weather was suitable. A flag flew to show that all was well, to save playgoers a wasted journey.

*Interior of the Swan Theatre – from a pen and ink drawing made in 1596 (Mansell Collection)*

At the entrance, a doorkeeper collected one penny (about 60p in modern money) for admission to the 'pit' – a name taken from the old inn-yards, where bear-baiting and cock-fighting were popular sports. This was the minimum charge for seeing a play. The 'groundlings', as they were called, simply stood around the three sides of the stage, in the open air. Those who were better off could pay extra for a seat under cover. Stairs led from the pit to three tiers of galleries round the walls. The higher one went, the more one paid. The best seats cost one shilling (or £6 today). In theatres owned by speculators like Francis Langley and Philip Henslowe, half the gallery takings went to the landlord.

A full house might consist of 800 groundlings and 1500 in the galleries, with a dozen more exclusive seats on the stage itself for the gentry. A new play might run for between six and sixteen performances; the average was about ten. As there were no breaks between scenes, and no intervals, most plays could be performed in two hours. A trumpet sounded three times before the play began.

The acting company assembled in the Tiring House at the rear of the stage. This was where they 'attired' (or dressed) themselves: not in costumes representing the period of the play, but in Elizabethan doublet and hose. All performances were therefore in modern dress, though no expense was spared to make the stage costumes lavish. The entire company was male. By law actresses were not allowed, and female roles were performed by boys.

Access to the stage from the Tiring House was through two doors, one on each side of the stage. Because there was no front curtain, every entrance had to have its corresponding exit, so an actor killed on stage had to be carried off. There was no scenery: the audience used its imagination, guided by the spoken word. Storms and night scenes might well be performed on sunny days in mid-afternoon; the Elizabethan playgoer relied entirely on the playwright's descriptive skills to establish the dramatic atmosphere.

Once on stage, the actors and their expensive clothes were protected from sudden showers by a canopy, the underside of which was painted blue, and spangled with stars to represent the heavens. A trapdoor in the stage made ghostly entrances and the gravedigging scene in *Hamlet* possible. Behind the main stage, in between the two entrance doors, there was a curtained area, concealing a small inner stage, useful for bedroom scenes. Above this was a balcony, which served for castle walls (as in *Henry V*) or a domestic balcony (as in the famous scene in *Romeo and Juliet*).

The acting style in Elizabethan times was probably more declamatory than we favour today, but the close proximity of the audience also made a degree of intimacy possible. In those days soliloquies and asides seemed quite natural. Act and scene divisions did not exist (those in printed versions of the play today have been added by editors), but Shakespeare often indicates a scene-ending by a rhyming couplet.

A company such as The King's Men at *The Globe* would consist of around twenty-five actors, half of whom might be shareholders, and the rest part-timers engaged for a particular play. Amongst the shareholders in *The Globe* were several specialists – William Kempe, for example, was a renowned comedian and Robert Armin was a singer and dancer. Playwrights wrote parts to suit the actors who were available, and devised ways of overcoming the absence of women. Shakespeare often has his heroines dress as young men, and physical contact between lovers was formal compared with the realism we expect today.

## His verse

Shakespeare wrote his plays mostly in blank verse: that is, unrhymed lines consisting of ten syllables, alternately stressed and unstressed. The technical term for this form is the 'iambic pentameter'. When Shakespeare first began to write for the

13

stage, it was fashionable to maintain this regular beat from the first line of the play till the last.

Shakespeare conformed at first, and then experimented. Some of his early plays contain whole scenes in rhyming couplets – in *Romeo and Juliet*, for example, there is extensive use of rhyme, and as if to show his versatility, Shakespeare even inserts a sonnet into the dialogue.

But as he matured, he sought greater freedom of expression than rhyme allowed. Rhyme is still used to indicate a scene-ending, or to stress lines which he wishes the audience to remember. Generally, though, Shakespeare moved towards the rhythms of everyday speech. This gave him many dramatic advantages, which he fully and subtly exploits in terms of atmosphere, character, emotion, stress and pace.

It is Shakespeare's poetic imagery, however, that most distinguishes his verse from that of lesser playwrights. It enables him to stretch the imagination, express complex thought-patterns in memorable language, and convey a number of associated ideas in a compressed and economical form. A study of Shakespeare's imagery – especially in his later plays – is often the key to a full understanding of his meaning and purposes.

At the other extreme is prose. Shakespeare normally reserves it for servants, clowns, commoners, and pedestrian matters such as lists, messages and letters.

# Romeo and Juliet

## Date

*Romeo and Juliet* was probably written and first acted in 1595. Shakespeare's company was at that time performing at *The Theatre*, in Shoreditch, as The Lord Chamberlain's Men. The play was first published in a pirated quarto edition in 1597. In 1599, a second quarto appeared, 'newly corrected, augmented and amended'. This 'good' quarto was reprinted ten years later.

## Source

There were many versions of the Romeo and Juliet story in European circulation in the fifteenth and sixteenth centuries. In England it became known through Arthur Brooke's 3,000 line poem *The Tragical Historie of Romeo and Juliet*, published in 1562. According to Brooke (whose own source was French) there was already a stage version in existence, but the text has not survived. In 1567 William Painter included the Romeo and Juliet story in his anthology *The Palace of Pleasure*, which went into a second edition in 1580.

There is little doubt that Shakespeare had the Brooke poem at his side as he worked on his play. It provided him with most of his raw material: the basic plot, and many of the characters. Some lines and speeches have strong echoes of the original poem, and Shakespeare relied on it for his understanding of life in Verona, its climate, and its general atmosphere. The finished product, of course, is entirely his own creation. New characters are invented or developed; the action is compressed; and the play has a lyrical and emotional intensity in the development and interrelationship of its themes, and in its language.

## Text

The first, 'bad' quarto of 1597 was not printed from Shakespeare's own manuscript. It was probably put together from several sources: actors' parts, the notes of speedwriters who attended performances, and passages reconstructed from memory. The second 'good' quarto of 1599 is considerably longer, and seems to have been based on what Shakespeare actually wrote and intended for publication. A comparison of the two quartos suggests, however, that the 1599 printer had a copy of the 1597 publication for guidance, and that he occasionally used it.

Modern editors mostly follow the second quarto, but not slavishly. Decisions have to be made: whether to print certain passages as prose or verse; whether to choose this word rather than that; whether to delete or correct or ignore what appear to be printers' errors or misunderstandings. In the case of *Romeo and Juliet* there are many such problems. Texts therefore vary.

# Romeo and Juliet

Original text and modern version

# The characters

**Escalus**   Prince of Verona
**Paris**   a young Count, kinsman to the Prince
**Montague** ⎫
**Capulet** ⎭ heads of two feuding houses
**An Old Man**   Capulet's kinsman
**Romeo**   Montague's son
**Mercutio**   kinsman to the Prince, and friend to Romeo
**Benvolio**   nephew to Montague, and friend to Romeo
**Tybalt**   nephew to Lady Capulet
**Friar Lawrence** ⎫
**Friar John** ⎭ of the Franciscan order
**Balthazar**   servant to Romeo
**Sampson** ⎫
**Gregory** ⎪
**Antony** ⎬ servants to Capulet
**Potpan** ⎭
**Peter**   servant to Juliet's Nurse
**Abraham**   servant to Montague
**An Apothecary**
**Three Musicians**
**Page to Paris; another Page; an Officer**
**Lady Montague**   wife to Montague
**Lady Capulet**   wife to Capulet
**Juliet**   daughter to Capulet
**Nurse to Juliet**
**Citizens of Verona;   Kinsfolk of both houses; Maskers, Guards**
**Watchmen and Attendants**
**Chorus**

# The Prologue

*Enter* **Chorus**

**Chorus**   Two households both alike in dignity,
In fair Verona where we lay our scene
From ancient grudge, break to new mutiny,
Where civil blood makes civil hands unclean:
5   From forth the fatal loins of these two foes,
A pair of star-crossed lovers take their life:
Whose misadventured piteous overthrows,
Doth with their death bury their parents' strife.
The fearful passage of their death-marked love,
10   And the continuance of their parents' rage,
Which but their children's end nought could remove,
Is now the two hours' traffic of our stage.
The which if you with patient ears attend,
What here shall miss, our toil shall strive to mend.

## The Prologue

*Before the play begins, an* **Announcer** *addresses the audience.*

**Announcer**   The play is set in beautiful Verona, in Italy. Two
families of equal, noble rank [*the Montagues and Capulets*],
have a long-standing vendetta, which has recently flared up:
their followers have killed each other in civil strife. The
children of these mortal enemies were fated to fall in love;
their tragic deaths ended their parents' feud.

The subject of our two-hour play is the harrowing story of
their fatal love-affair, the course of their parents' quarrel, and
the way in which it could only be ended by their deaths.

If you will give us your patient attention, we'll make up for
any shortcomings by performing as well as we can.

# Act one

## Scene 1

*Enter* **Sampson** *and* **Gregory** *with swords and bucklers of the house of Capulet*

**Sampson**    Gregory, on my word we'll not carry coals.

**Gregory**    No, for then we should be colliers.

**Sampson**    I mean, and we be in choler, we'll draw.

**Gregory**    Ay while you live, draw your neck out of collar.

5 **Sampson**    I strike quickly being moved.

**Gregory**    But thou art not quickly moved to strike.

**Sampson**    A dog of the house of Montague moves me.

**Gregory**    To move is to stir, and to be valiant is to stand: therefore if thou art moved, thou runn'st away.

10 **Sampson**    A dog of that house shall move me to stand: I will take the wall of any man or maid of Montague's.

**Gregory**    That shows thee a weak slave, for the weakest goes to the wall.

**Sampson**    'Tis true, and therefore women being the weaker
15 vessels are ever thrust to the wall; therefore I will push Montague's men from the wall, and thrust his maids to the wall.

# Act one

## Scene 1

*As he leaves, the play begins with the entry of* **Sampson** *and* **Gregory***, two servants of the Capulet family. They are armed with swords and small shields, and look ready for trouble.*

**Sampson**   They'll not rub our noses in the dirt, Gregory, believe me!

**Gregory**   No – 'cos then we'd be as mucky as miners . . .

**Sampson**   I mean, if we get hot under the collar, we'll fight!
[*He grips his sword, to show he is ready to draw it*]

**Gregory**   [*agreeing*] Oh, ay. Don't put your neck in a noose. It would be more than your life's worth . . .

5 **Sampson**   I strike out quickly, once my blood boils.

**Gregory**   But it is not easily roused . . .

**Sampson**   One of those Montague dogs always gets me going!

**Gregory**   'To get going' means 'to bestir yourself'. 'To be brave' means 'to stand your ground'. If you get going, you'll be running away!

10 **Sampson**   One of those dogs will certainly get me going. And I'll stand my ground, too! No man or woman of Montague's would make me step into the gutter!

**Gregory**   That shows what a feeble fellow you are. The weakest always goes to the wall.

**Sampson**   That's true. That's why women, being the weaker
15 sex, are always backed against walls! I'll push Montague's men into the roadway, and thrust his girls against the wall!

**Gregory**    The quarrel is between our masters, and us their men.

20 **Sampson**    'Tis all one. I will show myself a tyrant; when I have fought with the men, I will be civil with the maids, I will cut off their heads.

**Gregory**    The heads of the maids?

**Sampson**    Ay, the heads of the maids, or their maidenheads; 25    take it in what sense thou wilt.

**Gregory**    They must take it in sense that feel it.

**Sampson**    Me they shall feel while I am able to stand, and 'tis known I am a pretty piece of flesh.

**Gregory**    'Tis well thou are not fish; if thou hadst, thou hadst 30    been poor John: draw thy tool, here comes two of the house of Montagues.

[*Enter two other Servingmen,* **Abraham** *and* **Balthazar**]

**Sampson**    My naked weapon is out: quarrel, I will back thee.

**Gregory**    How, turn thy back and run?

**Sampson**    Fear me not.

35 **Gregory**    No marry; I fear thee.

**Sampson**    Let us take the law of our sides; let them begin.

**Gregory**    I will frown as I pass by, and let them take it as they list.

**Sampson**    Nay, as they dare. I will bite my thumb at them, 40    which is disgrace to them if they bear it.

**Gregory**    [*unhappy about the morality of this*] But the feud is only between our masters, and us their men . . .

**Sampson**    It's all the same to me. I'll be a right villain! When I've fought all the men, I'll be genteel with the maids. I'll cut their heads off.

**Gregory**    [*aghast*] The heads of the maids?

**Sampson**    Yes – the heads of the maids, or their maidenheads! Take it in whichever sense you please.

**Gregory**    Those who sense it, should feel it!

**Sampson**    So long as I can stand erect, they'll feel me! I'm well known for my meat!

**Gregory**    Fortunately, not for your fish: you'd make a poor catch! [*He sees two Montague men approach, and unsheaths his sword in readiness for trouble.*] Draw your tool. Here come two of Montague's people.

[**Abraham** *enters with a fellow-servant* **Balthazar**]

**Sampson**    My naked weapon is out. Quarrel with them. I'll back you up.

**Gregory**    How d'you mean? Turn and run?

**Sampson**    Have no fear!

**Gregory**    No indeed. Not of you!

**Sampson**    Let's have the law on our side. Let them make the first move.

**Gregory**    I'll frown as I pass them. They can take it whichever way they please.

**Sampson**    Or dare, even. I'll thumb my nose at them. They'll be shamed if they put up with that. [*He makes a quick rude gesture*]

**Abraham**    Do you bite your thumb at us sir?

**Sampson**    I do bite my thumb sir.

**Abraham**    Do you bite your thumb at us sir?

**Sampson**    Is the law of our side if I say ay?

45 **Gregory**    No.

**Sampson**    No sir, I do not bite my thumb at you sir, but I bite my thumb sir.

**Gregory**    Do you quarrel sir?

**Abraham**    Quarrel sir, no sir.

50 **Sampson**    But if you do sir, I am for you; I serve as good a man as you.

**Abraham**    No better.

**Sampson**    Well sir.

[*Enter* **Benvolio**]

**Gregory**    Say better: here comes one of my master's kinsmen.

55 **Sampson**    Yes, better sir.

**Abraham**    You lie.

**Sampson**    Draw if you be men. Gregory, remember thy washing blow.

[*They fight*]

**Abraham**    [*with forced politeness*] Did you thumb your nose at us, sir?

**Sampson**    I thumbed my nose . . .

**Abraham**    [*very deliberately*] Did you thumb your nose at us, sir?

**Sampson**    [*seeking* **Gregory**'s *advice*] Is the law on our side if I say yes?

**Gregory**    No.

**Sampson**    No, sir. I didn't thumb my nose at you, sir. But I did thumb my nose . . .

**Gregory**    Are you looking for trouble, sir?

**Abraham**    Trouble, sir? No, sir.

**Sampson**    'Cos if you are, sir, I'm ready for you. I serve as good a man as you do.

**Abraham**    No better?

**Sampson**    [*sensing a trap*] Well, sir . . .

[**Benvolio**, *a Montague, comes into view.* **Tybalt,** *a Capulet, is close behind him*]

**Gregory**    [*whispering*] Say 'better' – here's one of our master's relatives.

**Sampson**    Yes. Better, sir.

**Abraham**    You liar!

**Sampson**    Draw your swords, if you call yourselves men. Gregory, remember your swashing stroke! [*He demonstrates with a swish of his sword through the air*]

[**Benvolio** *is dismayed. He rushes in with raised sword*]

27

**Benvolio**    Part fools.
60      Put up your swords, you know not what you do.

[*Enter* **Tybalt**]

**Tybalt**    What, art thou drawn among these hartless hinds?
Turn thee Benvolio, look upon they death.

**Benvolio**    I do but keep the peace; put up thy sword,
Or manage it to part these men with me.

65    **Tybalt**    What, drawn and talk of peace? I hate the word
As I hate hell, all Montagues, and thee.
Have at thee coward!

[*They fight*]

[*Enter three or four* **Citizens** *with clubs or partisans*]

**Officer**    Clubs, bills and partisans, strike, beat them down!
Down with the Capulets, down with the Montagues!

[*Enter old* **Capulet** *and* **Lady Capulet**]

70    **Capulet**    What noise is this? Give me my long sword, ho!

**Lady Capulet**    A crutch, a crutch; why call you for a sword?

**Capulet**    My sword I say! Old Montague is come,
And flourishes his blade in spite of me.

[*Enter old* **Montague** *and* **Lady Montague**]

75    **Montague**    Thou villain Capulet: hold me not, let me go.

**Lady Montague**    Thou shalt not stir one foot to seek a foe.

[*Enter* **Prince Escalus** *with his train*]

**Benvolio**    Break it up, you fools! You don't know what you are doing!

**Tybalt**    What, are you mixing in a brawl with servants? Turn, Benvolio, and face your death!

**Benvolio**    I'm only trying to keep the peace; put back your sword, or use it to help me part these men.

**Tybalt**    What – talking of peace with your sword drawn? I hate the word: like I hate hell, all Montagues – and you! [*He makes a thrust at* **Benvolio**] Come on, then, coward!

[*They fight. Three or four* **Citizens** *join in*]

**Citizens**    Clubs! Battleaxes! Spears! Strike out! Beat 'em down! [*Some*] Down with the Capulets! [*Others*] Down with the Montagues!

[**Old Capulet** *enters in his nightgown, with* **Lady Capulet**, *his wife*]

**Capulet**    What's all this noise? [*Calling to his servants*] Give me my long sword, there!

**Lady Capulet**    [*mocking his advanced age*] A crutch, more like it! A crutch! Why ask for a sword?

**Capulet**    My sword, I say! Old Montague is coming, waving his sword about to provoke me!

[*Old* **Montague** *enters with* **Lady Montague**]

**Montague**    You villain, Capulet! [**Lady Montague** *tries to restrain him*] Don't hold me back! Let me go!

**Lady Montague**    Not one single foot towards an enemy!

[**Prince Escalus** *of Verona and his men appear on the scene*]

**Prince**   Rebellious subjects, enemies to peace,
Profaners of this neighbour-stained steel –
Will they not hear? What ho, you men, you beasts
That quench the fire of your pernicious rage
80   With purple fountains issuing from your veins:
On pain of torture, from those bloody hands,
Throw your mistempered weapons to the ground,
And hear the sentence of your moved Prince.
Three civil brawls bred of an airy word,
85   By thee old Capulet and Montague,
Have thrice disturbed the quiet of our streets,
And made Verona's ancient citizens
Cast by their grave beseeming ornaments
To wield old partisans, in hands as old,
90   Cankered with peace, to part your cankered hate.
If ever you disturb our streets again
Your lives shall pay the forfeit of the peace.
For this time all the rest depart away;
You, Capulet, shall go along with me,
95   And Montague, come you this afternoon,
To know our farther pleasure in this case,
To old Freetown, our common judgement-place.
Once more, on pain of death, all men depart.

[*Exeunt all but* **Montague, Lady Montague** *and* **Benvolio**]

**Montague**   Who set this ancient quarrel new abroach?
100   Speak, nephew, were you by when it began?

**Benvolio**   Here were the servants of your adversary
And yours, close fighting ere I did approach.
I drew to part them; in the instant came
The fiery Tybalt, with his sword prepared,
105   Which, as he breathed defiance to my ears
He swung about his head and cut the winds,
Who nothing hurt withal, hissed him in scorn.

**Prince**    Rebels! Peacebreakers! [*His voice is lost in the din*]
Neighbour-killers! [*The two sides fight on regardless*] Are
they deaf? [*Raising his voice*] You there! You men there! You
beasts! Cooling your ardour with your own spilt blood! On
pain of torture: drop those misused weapons from your
bloodstained hands and listen to the verdict of your angry
Prince! [*The fighting stops*] Three times the peace of our
streets has been disturbed by brawling citizens, and all
because of some trifling remark by you, old Capulet, and you,
Montague. Our older folk have put aside their sober habits
and brandished in their aged hands weapons rusted with
disuse, to come between you in your cancerous hatred. If ever
you breach the peace again your lives will pay the price. For
now, let the crowd disperse. You Capulet, will go along with
me. You, Montague, must come this afternoon to my court at
Old Freetown, to hear what else I have to say about the matter.
Once more – on pain of death – disperse!

[*They all leave sheepishly, except* **Montague, Lady Montague**
*and* **Benvolio**]

**Montague**    Who started all this off again? [*To* **Benvolio**] Tell us,
nephew: were you here when it began?

**Benvolio**    Your enemy's servants were fighting hand-to-hand
with yours before I came. I drew my sword to separate them.
At that very point the hot-headed Tybalt arrived, his sword
already out. He swung it round his head, shouted abuse at me,
and scythed the air which, not being hurt, merely swished and

While we were interchanging thrusts and blows
Came more and more, and fought on part and part,
110    Till the Prince came, who parted either part.

**Lady Montague**    O where is Romeo, saw you him today?
Right glad I am he was not at this fray.

**Benvolio**    Madam, an hour before the worshipped sun
Peered forth the golden window of the east
115    A troubled mind drive me to walk abroad,
Where underneath the grove of sycamore
That westward rooteth from this city side,
So early walking did I see your son.
Towards him I made, but he was ware of me,
120    And stole into the covert of the wood.
I, measuring his affections by my own,
Which then most sought, where most might not be found,
Being one too many by my weary self,
Pursued my humour, not pursuing his,
125    And gladly shunned who gladly fled from me.

**Montague**    Many a morning hath he there been seen,
With tears augmenting the fresh morning's dew,
Adding to clouds more clouds with his deep sighs;
But all so soon as the all-cheering sun
130    Should in the farthest east begin to draw
The shady curtains from Aurora's bed,
Away from light steals home my heavy son
And private in his chamber pens himself,
Shuts up his windows, locks fair daylight out
135    And makes himself an artificial night.
Black and portentous must this humour prove
Unless good counsel may the cause remove.

**Benvolio**    My noble uncle, do you know the cause?

**Montague**    I neither know it nor can learn of him.

140 **Benvolio**    Have you importuned him by any means?

hissed in scorn. While we were exchanging cuts and thrusts, others came, and fought in pairs, till the Prince came and separated them.

**Lady Montague** Where is Romeo? Have you seen him today? I'm very glad he wasn't involved in this affray.

**Benvolio** Madam, an hour before sunrise, a restlessness of mind led me to go for a walk. Beneath a sycamore grove that grows to the west of this side of the city, I saw your son taking an early stroll. I made towards him, but knowing I was there, he hid within the wood. Judging his feelings by my own – what I wanted most was a place where fewest people were to be found: even my own weary company was one too many – I indulged my whim by not enquiring about his. I gladly avoided my avoider.

**Montague** He's often been seen there of a morning, his tears supplementing the morning dew, his deep sighs forming new clouds with his breath. But once the cheerful sun starts rising in the east, to dodge the light my gloomy son steals home. He confines himself alone to his room, shutters his windows, locks out daylight, and makes an artificial night for himself. This mood is sinister and alarming, unless the cause can be removed by means of good advice.

**Benvolio** Noble uncle, do you know the cause?

**Montague** I neither know it, nor can find it out from him.

**Benvolio** Have you questioned him at all?

**Montague**    Both by myself and many other friends.
But he, his own affections' counsellor,
Is to himself – I will not say how true –
But to himself so secret and so close,
145    So far from sounding and discovery,
As is the bud bit with an envious worm
Ere he can spread his sweet leaves to the air
Or dedicate his beauty to the sun.
Could we but learn from whence his sorrows grow,
150    We would as willingly give cure as know.

[*Enter* **Romeo**]

**Benvolio**    See where he comes. So please you step aside;
I'll know his grievance or be much denied.

**Montague**    I would thou wert so happy by thy stay
To hear true shrift. Come, madam, let's away.

[*Exeunt* **Montague** *and* **Lady Montague**]

**Benvolio**    Good morrow, cousin.

155  **Romeo**                                        Is the day so young?

**Benvolio**    But new struck nine.

**Romeo**                                      Ay me, sad hours seem long.
Was that my father that went hence so fast?

**Benvolio**    It was. What sadness lengthens Romeo's hours?

**Romeo**    Not having that which, having, makes them short.

160  **Benvolio**    In love?

**Romeo**    Out.

**Benvolio**    Of love?

**Romeo**    Out of her favour where I am in love.

**Montague**   I have, and so have many other friends. But being so withdrawn, he's so secretive and close – I won't say 'true to himself' – that his thoughts are no more detectable than an ill-natured worm within a bud that hasn't opened or revealed its beauty. We're as anxious to cure his sorrows as we are to find the reason for them.

[**Romeo** *enters*]

**Benvolio**   Look, here he comes! Step to one side, if you would. I'll find out what's grieving him, unless he's very obstinate.

**Montague**   I hope you are duly rewarded with the truth. [*To his wife*] Come, madam. We'll go.

**Benvolio**   Good morning cousin.

**Romeo**   Is it so early?

**Benvolio**   It's just past nine.

**Romeo**   [*sighing deeply*] Oh, dear. Time drags when you're sad. Was that my father who went off so quickly?

**Benvolio**   It was. What's this sadness that makes time drag for you, Romeo?

**Romeo**   Not having what would make time fly, if it was mine.

**Benvolio**   In love?

**Romeo**   Out –

**Benvolio**   Of love?

**Romeo**   Out of favour with my loved one.

**Benvolio**    Alas that love so gentle in his view
165    Should be so tyrannous and rough in proof.

**Romeo**    Alas that love whose view is muffled still
Should without eyes see pathways to his will.
Where shall we dine? O me! What fray was here?
Yet tell me not, for I have heard it all.
170    Here's much to do with hate, but more with love.
Why then, O brawling love, O loving hate,
O anything of nothing first create!
O heavy lightness, serious vanity,
Misshapen chaos of well-seeming forms!
175    Feather of lead, bright smoke, cold fire, sick health,
Still-waking sleep that is not what it is!
This love feel I that feel no love in this.
Dost thou not laugh?

**Benvolio**                           No coz, I rather weep.

**Romeo**    Good heart, at what?

**Benvolio**                           At thy good heart's oppression.

180 **Romeo**    Why such is love's transgression.
Griefs of mine own lie heavy in my breast,
Which thou wilt propagate to have it pressed
With more of thine. This love that thou hast shown
Doth add more grief to too much of mine own.
185    Love is a smoke made with the fume of sighs;
Being purged, a fire sparkling in lovers' eyes;
Being vexed, a sea nourished with lovers' tears;
What is it else? A madness most discreet,
A choking gall, and a preserving sweet.
Farewell, my coz.

190 **Benvolio**                           Soft, I will go along;
And if you leave me so, you do me wrong.

**Romeo**    Tut, I have lost myself, I am not here.
This is not Romeo, he's some other where.

**Benvolio**    Alas, that Cupid, so gentle in appearance, should be
so dominating and inconsiderate in action!

**Romeo**    Alas that Cupid – in spite of his blindfold – should see
his objective so clearly! Where shall we have dinner? [*He
sighs again*] Oh, dear! What was the fighting about? Don't tell
me – I've heard all about it. It's got a lot to do with hate, but
more with love. [*We learn later why;* **Romeo,** *a Montague,
loves* **Rosaline,** *a Capulet. He indulges in some heavy self-
pity*] Oh, brawling love! Oh, loving hate! Nothing can come
from nothing! Oh, heavy lightheartedness! Weighty folly!
Things that look good are all a grotesque muddle!
Featherweight lead; bright smoke; cold fire; sick health; wide-
awake sleep, which isn't sleep at all! I'm in love, but it's not
returned . . . [*He looks at* **Benvolio** *self-consciously*] Are you
laughing?

**Benvolio**    No, cousin, weeping, rather.

**Romeo**    Dear fellow – what at?

**Benvolio**    At your heartache . . .

**Romeo**    That's the nature of love. My sorrows will increase, if
you graft your own to them. This love you've shown just adds
more grief to my plentiful stock. Love is a smoke, the fumes of
sighing. When it clears away, it's the sparkling fire in lovers'
eyes. Cross it, and it's a sea swollen with lovers' tears. What
else is it? A wise madness . . . A deadly poison . . . A healing
medicine . . . [*He tries to take his leave*] Farewell, cousin. [*He
makes to go*]

**Benvolio**    [*catching his sleeve*] Just a moment, I'll go with you.
You do me an injustice to leave me like that.

**Romeo**    Hm . . . I'm not myself. I'm not with you. This isn't
Romeo here – he's somewhere else.

**Benvolio**    Tell me in sadness who is that you love?

195 **Romeo**    What, shall I groan and tell thee?

**Benvolio**    Groan? Why no, but sadly tell me who.

**Romeo**    Bid a sick man in sadness make his will?
A word ill-urged to one that is so ill.
In sadness, cousin, I do love a woman.

200 **Benvolio**    I aimed so near when I supposed you loved.

**Romeo**    A right good markman! And she's fair I love.

**Benvolio**    A right fair mark, fair coz, is soonest hit.

**Romeo**    Well, in that hit you miss; she'll not be hit
With Cupid's arrow, she hath Dian's wit,
205 And in strong proof of chastity well armed
From love's weak childish bow she lives unharmed.
She will not stay the siege of loving terms
Nor bid th' encounter of assailing eyes
· Nor ope her lap to saint-seducing gold;
210 O she is rich in beauty, only poor
That when she dies, with beauty dies her store.

**Benvolio**    Then she hath sworn that she will still live chaste?

**Romeo**    She hath, and in that sparing makes huge waste.
But beauty starved with her severity
215 Cuts beauty off from all posterity.
She is too fair, too wise, wisely too fair,
To merit bliss by making me despair.
She hath forsworn to love, and in that vow
Do I live dead, that live to tell it now.

220 **Benvolio**    Be ruled by me, forget to think of her.

**Romeo**    O teach me how I should forget to think.

**Benvolio**   Seriously now. Who's the girl?

**Romeo**   What – shall I groan, and tell you?

**Benvolio**   Groan? Well, no – but tell me in all seriousness who it is.

**Romeo**   Ask a sick man to make his will, 'in all seriousness'? Not very tactful in the serious circumstances . . . Seriously, cousin: I'm in love with a woman.

**Benvolio**   [*drily*] I had that target in my mind when I assumed you were in love . . .

**Romeo**   Well aimed, then. And the one I love is beautiful.

**Benvolio**   A striking target is easiest to hit.

**Romeo**   You missed with that shot. She's proof against Cupid's arrows; she has the goddess Diana's wisdom. She's so well armoured in defence of her virginity that she can't be wounded by the little fellow's puny weapon. She can't be won by sweet love-talk. She's invulnerable to loving looks. She wouldn't sell herself, not even for the kind of money that would tempt a saint. Oh – she is rich in beauty! She's only poor in the sense that when she dies, her beauty and fertility will cease . . .

**Benvolio**   Then has she sworn never to marry?

**Romeo**   She has, and what a waste there is in saving herself like that! Her virginity denies all future generations of her beauty. It isn't fair that her beauty, her wisdom and her virtue, should win her a place in heaven at the expense of my suffering! She has vowed to deny herself love: and that vow means I must endure a living death.

**Benvolio**   Take my advice. Forget her.

**Romeo**   Teach me how to forget to think . . .

**Benvolio**    By giving liberty unto thine eyes:
Examine other beauties.

**Romeo**                              'Tis the way
To call hers, exquisite, in question more.
225  These happy masks that kiss fair ladies' brows,
Being black, puts us in mind they hide the fair.
He that is strucken blind cannot forget
The precious treasure of his eyesight lost.
Show me a mistress that is passing fair;
230  What doth her beauty serve but as a note
Where I may read who passed that passing fair?
Farewell, thou canst not teach me to forget.

**Benvolio**    I'll pay that doctrine or else die in debt.

[*Exeunt*]

## Scene 2

*Enter* **Capulet, County Paris** *and the* **Clown, Capulet's** *servant*

**Capulet**    But Montague is bound as well as I,
In penalty alike, and 'tis not hard I think
For men so old as we to keep the peace.

**Paris**    Of honourable reckoning are you both,
5  And pity 'tis you lived at odds so long.
But now my lord, what say you to my suit?

**Capulet**    But saying o'er what I have said before.
My child is yet a stranger in the world,
She hath not seen the change of fourteen years.
10  Let two more summers wither in their pride
Ere we may think her ripe to be a bride.

**Paris**    Younger than she are happy mothers made.

**Benvolio**    By letting your eyes roam. Look at other beautiful girls.

**Romeo**    That would only make me value her exquisite charms the more. The black fun-masks which beautiful ladies wear make us think of the fair charms that lie hidden. The blind man can never forget the inestimable value of his lost eyesight. Show me a lady who is extremely beautiful: of what significance is her beauty, except to remind me of one who exceeds her in loveliness ? Goodbye. You cannot teach me to forget.

**Benvolio**    I'll win my point, or die in the attempt!

[*Both go off*]


## Scene 2

*A street in Verona. Enter* **Capulet, Count Paris,** *the* **Clown,** *and a* **Servant**


**Capulet**    But Montague is bound over just as I am, and on the same terms. It shouldn't be hard, I think, for men as old as we are to keep the peace.

**Paris**    You are both men of honourable reputations. It's a pity you've lived at odds with each other for so long. [*Changing the subject*] But now, my lord: what have you to say about my request to marry your daughter?

**Capulet**    Only to repeat what I've said before. My child is very immature. She isn't yet fourteen. Let's think about marriage in a couple of years.

**Paris**    Girls younger than she is have made happy mothers.

   **Capulet**   And too soon marred are those so early made.
       Earth hath swallowed all my hopes but she;
15   She is the hopeful lady of my earth.
       But woo her, gentle Paris, get her heart,
       My will to her consent is but a part,
       And she agreed, within her scope of choice
       Lies my consent and fair according voice.
20   This night I hold an old accustomed feast
       Whereto I have invited many a guest
       Such as I love, and you among the store:
       One more, most welcome, makes my number more.
       At my poor house look to behold this night
25   Earth-treading stars that make dark heaven light.
       Such comfort as do lusty young men feel
       When well-apparelled April on the heel
       Of limping winter treads, even such delight
       Among fresh female buds shall you this night
30   Inherit at my house. Hear all, all see,
       And like her most whose merit most shall be;
       Which, on more view of many, mine, being one,
       May stand in number, though in reckoning none.
       Come, go with me.

     [*To the* **Clown**, *giving him a paper*]

                        Go sirrah, trudge about
35   Through fair Verona, find those persons out
       Whose names are written there, and to them say,
       My house and welcome on their pleasure stay.

            [*Exeunt* **Capulet** *and* **Paris**]

   **Clown**   Find them out whose names are written here! It is
40   written that the shoemaker should meddle with his yard, and
     the tailor with his last, the fisher with his pencil, and the

**Capulet**    'Soon married, soon marred.' All my other children
are dead. She is all the world to me. But court her, gentle Paris:
win her heart. My feelings take second place to hers. Once her
consent is obtained, my own willing agreement follows.
Tonight I'm holding a festive party, to which I've invited many
of my best friends, with yourself as a very welcome addition.
At my humble house, you can expect to see some heavenly
beauties. After winter's depression, you'll enjoy the spring
feeling amongst the young girls you'll meet at my house
tonight. Listen to them all. Look at them all. Fall for the girl
who has most merit. Perhaps, after seeing a wide selection,
my daughter may be number one, though they say 'one isn't a
number'! Come along with me. [*He takes* **Paris** *by the arm. To
the* **Clown,** *offering a paper*] Off you go. Trudge round Verona,
find the people whose names are written here. Tell them I
await the pleasure of their company.

[**Capulet** *and* **Paris** *leave*]

**Clown**    Find the people whose names are written here? [*He
scans it, then turns it one way and another. Obviously, he can't
read*] It's said that the shoemaker should stick to his ruler, the
tailor to his last, the fisherman to his paintbrush and the

painter with his nets, but I am sent to find those persons
whose names are here writ, and can never find what names
the writing person hath here writ. I must to the learned.
45.  In good time!

[*Enter* **Benvolio** *and* **Romeo**]

**Benvolio**   Tut man, one fire burns out another's burning,
One pain is lessened by another's anguish;
Turn giddy, and be holp by backward turning.
One desperate grief cures with another's languish;
50  Take thou some new infection to thy eye
And the rank poison of the old will die.

**Romeo**   Your plantain leaf is excellent for that.

**Benvolio**   For what, I pray thee?

**Romeo**                                   For your broken shin.

**Benvolio**   Why, Romeo, art thou mad?

55 **Romeo**   Not mad, but bound more than a madman is:
Shut up in prison, kept without my food,
Whipped and tormented and – good e'en, good fellow.

**Clown**   God gi' good e'en; I pray, sir, can you read?

**Romeo**   Ay, mine own fortune in my misery.

60 **Clown**   Perhaps you have learned it without book. But I pray
can you read anything you see?

**Romeo**   Ay, if I know the letters and the language.

**Clown**   Ye say honestly; rest you merry.

painter to his nets. Yet I'm sent to find the people whose names are written here, though I can't read the names the writer has written! I must ask someone who's educated. [*He sees* **Benvolio** *and* **Romeo** *approaching*] Well timed!

[**Benvolio** *and* **Romeo** *enter*]

**Benvolio**   Tut, man! Fire burns out fire. Pain here is lessened by pain there; stop giddiness by spinning in reverse; an inconsolable grief is cured by further sorrow. The antidote to your affected sight is the vision of some new love, to make you blind!

**Romeo**   [*Scorning such a remedy*] Plantain leaves are excellent for that . . .

**Benvolio**   For what, may I ask?

**Romeo**   Cut knees!

**Benvolio**   [*not understanding*] Have you gone mad, Romeo?

**Romeo**   No, not mad. But I'm in more of a strait-jacket than a lunatic is. I'm imprisoned. Starved. Whipped and tormented. And – [*he notices the* **Clown**] Good afternoon young man.

**Clown**   And a good afternoon to you. May I ask, sir, whether you can read?

**Romeo**   Yes – my own unhappy future from my present misery . . .

**Clown**   [*knowing a love-sick young man when he sees one*] Perhaps that's something you've learned 'by heart'? But, please – can you read anything you see?

**Romeo**   Yes, provided I know the alphabet and the language it's written in.

**Clown**   [*thinking this means* **Romeo** *can't read*] That's very frank. [*He turns to go*] Cheers!

**Romeo**    Stay, fellow, I can read. [*He reads the list*]

65    'Signor Martino and his wife and daughters;
County Anselm and his beauteous sisters;
The lady widow of Utruvio;
Signor Placentio and his lovely nieces;
Mercutio and his brother Valentine;
70    Mine uncle Capulet, his wife and daughters;
My fair niece Rosaline and Livia;
Signor Valentio and his cousin Tybalt;
Lucio and the lively Helena.'

A fair assembly. Whither should they come?

75 **Clown**    Up.

**Romeo**    Whither to supper?

**Clown**    To our house.

**Romeo**    Whose house?

**Clown**    My master's.

80 **Romeo**    Indeed, I should have asked you that before.

**Clown**    Now I'll tell you without asking. My master is the great
rich Capulet, and if you be not of the house of Montagues I
pray come and crush a cup of wine. Rest you merry.

[*Exit*]

**Benvolio**    At this same ancient feast of Capulet's
85    Sups the fair Rosaline, whom thou so loves,
With all the admired beauties of Verona.
Go thither, and with unattainted eye
Compare her face with some that I shall show,
And I will make thee think thy swan a crow.

90 **Romeo**    When the devout religion of mine eye
Maintains such falsehood, then turn tears to fires;
And those who, often drowned, could never die,

**Romeo**    [*calling him back*] Hold on. I can read. [*He reads the list*]

> Signor Martino, and his wife and daughters;
> Count Anselm and his beautiful sisters;
> Vitruvio's widow;
> Signor Placentio and his lovely nieces;
> Mercutio, and his brother Valentine;
> My fair neice Rosaline and Livia;
> My uncle Capulet, his wife and daughter;
> Signor Valentio and his cousin, Tybalt;
> Lucio and lively Helena.'

A promising guest-list! Where are they to come?

**Clown**    Up.

**Romeo**    Up where? To supper?

**Clown**    To our house.

**Romeo**    Whose house?

**Clown**    My master's.

**Romeo**    I should have asked you that in the first place!

**Clown**    Now I'll tell you without asking. My master is the great, rich Capulet. Provided you aren't one of the house of Montague, come and drink a glass of wine. 'Bye now!

[*The **Clown** leaves*]

**Benvolio**    The beautiful Rosaline that you love so much will dine at this feast of Capulet's, together with the most desirable beauties of Verona. Go to it, and with an unprejudiced eye, compare her looks with others that I'll show you. I'll make you think your swan is nothing better than a crow!

**Romeo**    If ever my eyes blaspheme like that, in contradiction of my faith, may my tears turn to fire! And – like heretics who are tested first by drowning – may they be burnt as liars! A girl

Transparent heretics, be burnt for liars.
One fairer than my love! The all-seeing sun
95    Ne'er saw her match, since first the world begun.

**Benvolio**    Tut, you saw her fair none else being by,
Herself poised with herself in either eye;
But in that crystal scales let there be weighed
Your lady's love against some other maid
100    That I will show you shining at this feast,
And she shall scant show well that now seems best.

**Romeo**    I'll go along, no such sight to be shown,
But to rejoice in splendour of mine own.

[*Exeunt*]

## Scene 3

*Capulet's house. Enter* **Lady Capulet** *and* **Nurse**

**Lady Capulet**    Nurse, where's my daughter? Call her forth to
me.

**Nurse**    Now by my maidenhead at twelve year old,
I bade her come. What, lamb! What, ladybird!
5    God forbid. Where's this girl? What, Juliet!

[*Enter* **Juliet**]

**Juliet**    How now, who calls?

**Nurse**                                Your mother.

**Juliet**    Madam, I am here, what is your will?

**Lady Capulet**    This is the matter. Nurse, give leave awhile,
We must talk in secret. Nurse, come back again,
10    I have remembered me, thou's hear our counsel.
Thou knowest my daughter's of a pretty age.

more beautiful than my Rosaline? The all-seeing sun has never seen her equal since the world began!

**Benvolio**   You thought she was beautiful because there was no one to compare her with. She was balanced in both your eyes only against herself. But use the same visual scales to weigh your lady-love against another girl whom I'll show you, radiant, at this feast, and she'll scarcely pass muster, though now she seems best.

**Romeo**   I'll go along, not to see what you describe, but to revel in pleasures of my own.

[*They go*]

## Scene 3

*A room in Capulet's house. Enter* **Lady Capulet** *and* **Nurse**

**Lady Capulet**   Nurse, where's my daughter? Call her to me!

**Nurse**   Now by my virginity at twelve years old, I told her to come! [*Calling*] What, lamb! What, ladybird! [*To herself*] God forbid anything's happened to her, wherever is she? [*calling*] What, Juliet!

**Juliet**   What's the matter? Who's calling?

**Nurse**   Your mother.

**Juliet**   Madam, I am here. What is your wish?

**Lady Capulet**   It's this. Nurse, leave us a moment, we must talk in secret. [**Nurse** *starts to leave*] Nurse, come back again. I've just remembered, you shall hear our discussion. You know my daughter is of an attractive age.

**Nurse**    Faith, I can tell her age unto an hour.

**Lady Capulet**    She's not fourteen.

**Nurse**                                      I'll lay fourteen of my teeth,
And yet, to my teen be it spoken, I have but four,
15    She's not fourteen. How long is it now to
To Lammas-tide?

**Lady Capulet**          A fortnight and odd days.

**Nurse**    Even or odd, of all days in the year,
Come Lammas Eve at night shall she be fourteen.
Susan and she – God rest all Christian souls –
20    Were of an age. Well, Susan is with God:
She was too good for me. But as I said,
On Lammas Eve at night shall she be fourteen.
That shall she. Marry, I remember it well.
'Tis since the earthquake now eleven years,
25    And she was weaned – I never shall forget it –
Of all the days of the year upon that day.
For I had then laid wormwood to my dug,
Sitting in the sun under the dovehouse wall.
My lord and you were then at Mantua –
30    Nay I do bear a brain. But as I said,
When it did taste the wormwood on the nipple
Of my dug and felt it bitter, pretty fool,
To see it tetchy and fall out with the dug.
Shake! quoth the dovehouse. 'Twas no need, I trow,
35    To bid me trudge.
And since that time it is eleven years.
For then she could stand high-lone, nay, by th' rood,
She could have run and waddled all about;
For even the day before she broke her brow,
40    And then my husband, God be with his soul,
A was a merry man, took up the child,
'Yea', quoth he, 'dost thou fall upon thy face?

**Nurse**    Indeed, I can tell her age to the very hour.

**Lady Capulet**    She's not fourteen . . .

**Nurse**    I'll bet fourteen of my teeth – though to my sorrow I've only got four – that she's not fourteen! How far off is Lammas Day?

**Lady Capulet**    A fortnight and a few odd days.

**Nurse**    Even or odd, of all days of the year, on Lammas Eve, the night of 31 July, she'll be fourteen. Susan and she, God rest all Christian souls, were the same age. Well, Susan is with God; she was too good for me. But as I said, on Lammas Eve at night she'll be fourteen. That she will. O yes, I remember it well. It's eleven years now since that earthquake, and she was weaned – I shall never forget it – of all days of the year, on that very day. I'd just put some wormwood on my breast, sitting in the sun under the wall of the dovecote. My master and you were then in Mantua – what a memory I've got! But as I said: when she tasted the wormwood on the nipple and found it bitter: the pretty little thing, to see it so cross and out of friends with the breast! The dove-house started to shake. There was no need to tell me to be off, to be sure! That was eleven years ago, 'cos she could stand on her own by then. Indeed, by the Holy Cross, she could run and toddle around! Just the day before, she cut her head, and then my husband – God rest his soul, he was full of fun! – he lifted the child up. 'Yes,' he said. 'Did you fall on your face?' You'll fall on your back when you've got

Thou wilt fall backward when thou hast more wit,
Wilt thou not, Jule?' And by my holidame,
45   The pretty wretch left crying and said 'Ay'.
To see now how a jest shall come about.
I warrant, and I should live a thousand years
I never should forget it. 'Wilt thou not, Jule?' quoth he,
And, pretty fool, it stinted, and said 'Ay'.

50 **Lady Capulet**   Enough of this, I pray thee, hold thy peace.

**Nurse**   Yes, madam, yet I cannot choose but laugh
To think it should leave crying and say 'Ay'.
And yet I warrant it had upon its brow
A bump as big as a young cockerel's stone,
55   A perilous knock, and it cried bitterly.
'Yea', quoth my husband, 'fall'st upon thy face?
Thou wilt fall backward when thou comest to age,
Wilt thou not, Jule?' It stinted, and said 'Ay'.

**Juliet**   And stint thou too, I pray thee, Nurse, say I.

60 **Nurse**   Peace, I have done. God mark thee to his grace,
Thou wast the prettiest babe that e'er I nursed.
And I might live to see thee married once,
I have my wish.

**Lady Capulet**   Marry, that marry is the very theme
65   I came to talk of. Tell me, daughter Juliet,
How stands your dispositions to be married?

**Juliet**   It is an honour that I dream not of.

**Nurse**   An honour! Were not I thine only nurse
I would say thou hadst sucked wisdom from thy teat.

70 **Lady Capulet**   Well, think of marriage now. Younger than
      you
Here in Verona, ladies of esteem,
Are made already mothers. By my count

more sense, won't you Jule?' And by all that's holy, the pretty brat stopped crying and said 'Yes'! Fancy how a joke should come so true! I swear that if I lived a thousand years, I'd never forget it. 'Won't you, Jule?' he said. And the pretty chick just stopped crying, and said 'Yes'! [*The* **Nurse** *enjoys the story hugely, and rocks with laughter*]

**Lady Capulet**   That's enough. Quiet, now.

**Nurse**   [*not easily switched off*] Yes madam. But I can't stop laughing to think it should stop crying and say 'Yes'! Though I'll swear it had a bump on its brow as big as a young cockerel's balls – a nasty bump – and it cried bitterly. 'Yes,' said my husband. 'Did you fall on your face? You'll fall on your back when you grow up, won't you, Jule?' [*She is in hysterics now*] It stopped crying and said 'Yes'!

**Juliet**   I do wish you'd stop, Nurse, please!

**Nurse**   [*controlling herself*] Right. I've finished. God love you, you were the prettiest baby I ever nursed. If I could just see you married, I'd have my wish.

**Lady Capulet**   Marriage is the very theme I came to talk about. Tell me, daughter Juliet, how do you feel about getting married?

**Juliet**   It's an honour I don't dream about.

**Nurse**   An honour! If I weren't your only nurse, I'd say you'd sucked wisdom at the breast!

**Lady Capulet**   Well, think about marriage now. Here in Verona, many well-bred ladies younger than you are already mothers. By my reckoning, I was your mother just about your present

I was your mother much upon these years
75  That you are now a maid. Thus then in brief:
The valiant Paris seeks you for his love.

**Nurse**   A man, young lady! Lady, such a man
As all the world – why, he's a man of wax.

**Lady Capulet**   Verona's summer hath not such a flower.

80  **Nurse**   Nay, he's a flower, in faith a very flower.

**Lady Capulet**   What say you, can you love the gentleman?
This night you shall behold him at our feast;
Read o'er the volume of young Paris' face
And find delight writ there with beauty's pen.
85  Examine every married lineament
And see how one another lends content;
And what obscured in this fair volume lies,
Find written in the margent of his eyes.
This precious book of love, this unbound lover,
90  To beautify him only lacks a cover.
The fish lives in the sea; and 'tis much pride
For fair without the fair within to hide.
That book in many's eyes doth share the glory
That in gold clasps locks in the golden story.
95  So shall you share all that he doth possess,
By having him, making yourself no less.

**Nurse**   No less, nay bigger. Women grow by men.

**Lady Capulet**   Speak briefly, can you like of Paris' love?

**Juliet**   I'll look to like, if looking liking move,
100  But no more deep will I endart mine eye
Than your consent gives strength to make it fly.

[*Enter a* **Servingman**]

age. In short, the worthy Paris seeks you as his bride.

**Nurse**    [*overjoyed*] A man, young lady! Lady, such a man as the entire world – [*she can't find words adequate to describe him*] why – he's *perfect*!

**Lady Capulet**    He has no equal, not even amongst Verona's summer flowers.

**Nurse**    Yes – he's a flower. A real flower!

**Lady Capulet**    What do you say? Can you love the gentleman? You'll see him tonight at our feast. Scan Paris's face as if it were a book. Attractiveness is the central theme. Examine every feature and see how the contents combine together to make a congenial whole. Should anything in this fine volume be obscure, consult his eyes for an explanation. This great love-story, this romance that's waiting for a dedication, lacks one thing only; a cover. Just as the sea surrounds the fish, so a beautiful woman is the wrapper round a handsome man. When a book with a romantic story is locked with golden clasps, many people think its attractiveness is thereby shared. Likewise, by marrying Paris, you'll share all his attributes – and your own will be no less.

**Nurse**    No less? Nay, bigger! Men make women pregnant!

**Lady Capulet**    A short answer: do you like the idea of Paris's love?

**Juliet**    If looking leads to liking, I expect I shall. But I won't commit myself any further than you want me to.

[*A* **Servant** *runs on*]

**Servingman**   Madam, the guests are come, supper served up,
you called, my young lady asked for, the Nurse cursed in
the pantry, and everything in extremity. I must hence to wait,
105   I beseech you follow straight.

[*Exit*]

**Lady Capulet**   We follow thee. Juliet, the County stays.

**Nurse**   Go, girl, seek happy nights to happy days.

[*Exeunt*]

## Scene 4

*A street. Enter* **Romeo, Mercutio, Benvolio,** *with five or six other*
**Masquers** *and* **Torchbearers**

**Romeo**   What, shall this speech be spoke for our excuse?
Or shall we on without apology?

**Benvolio**   The date is out of such prolixity.
We'll have no Cupid hoodwinked with a scarf,
5   Bearing a Tartar's painted bow of lath,
Scaring the ladies like a crowkeeper,
Nor no without-book prologue, faintly spoke
After the prompter, for our entrance.
But let them measure us by what they will,
10   We'll measure them a measure and be gone.

**Romeo**   Give me a torch, I am not for this ambling.
Being but heavy I will bear the light.

**Mercutio**   Nay, gentle Romeo, we must have you dance.

**Servant**   [*Breathless*] Madam, the guests have arrived – supper is served – they're waiting for you and asking for my young lady – the nurse is being cursed in the pantry – and everything's in a muddle! I must go and serve at table. Please come at once!

**Lady Capulet**   We'll follow you. Juliet, the Count is waiting for you.

**Nurse**   Off you go, girl: aim for happy nights to make sure of happy days!

## Scene 4

*Evening, outside Capulet's house.* **Romeo, Mercutio, Benvolio** *and several other masked men enter, led by* **Torchbearers** *lighting the way*

**Romeo**   [*a scroll is in his hand*] Shall we deliver the usual formal speech, or just intrude without apology?

**Benvolio**   Rigmaroles like that are old-fashioned. Let's have none of this blindfolded-Cupid business: being led in by a fellow carrying a wooden oriental sword, and frightening the ladies like a walking scarecrow. And none of those badly-memorised prologues, delivered in a faint voice with help from a prompter, to make our entrances. Let them take us how they will. We'll do our dance for them, then go.

**Romeo**   Give me a torch to carry instead. I'm not one for this kind of prancing. I'll hold the light, seeing I'm so heavy-hearted.

**Mercutio**   No, Romeo, we must have you dancing!

**Romeo**    Not I, believe me. You have dancing shoes
15    With nimble soles, I have a soul of lead
So stakes me to the ground I cannot move.

**Mercutio**    You are a lover, borrow Cupid's wings
And soar with them above a common bound.

**Romeo**    I am too sore enpierced with his shaft
20    To soar with his light feathers, and so bound
I cannot bound a pitch above dull woe.
Under love's heavy burden do I sink.

**Mercutio**    And, to sink in it, should you burden love –
Too great oppression for a tender thing.

25 **Romeo**    Is love a tender thing? It is too rough,
Too rude, too boisterous, and it pricks like a thorn.

**Mercutio**    If love be rough with you, be rough with love;
Prick love for pricking and you beat love down.
Give me a case to put my visage in:
30    A visor for a visor. What care I
What curious eye doth quote deformities?
Here are the beetle brows shall blush for me.

**Benvolio**    Come, knock and enter, and no sooner in
But every man betake him to his legs.

35 **Romeo**    A torch for me. Let wantons light of heart
Tickle the senseless rushes with their heels,
For I am proverbed with a grandsire phrase –
I'll be a candle-holder and look on.
The game was ne'er so fair, and I am dun.

40 **Mercutio**    Tut, dun's the mouse, the constable's own word.
If thou art Dun we'll draw thee from the mire
Of – save your reverence – love, wherein thou stickest
Up to the ears. Come, we burn daylight, ho.

**Romeo**   Not me, I assure you. You have dancing shoes with light soles – I have a heavy-as-lead soul, that fixes me to the ground so I can't move.

**Mercutio**   You're in love. Borrow Cupid's wings, and soar into the sky!

**Romeo**   I'm too sore with his arrow-wound to soar with flimsy wings like his. I'm so pinned down, I couldn't jump higher than the depths of misery. I'm sunk beneath love's weight.

**Mercutio**   'Sinking down' makes love a burden – far too heavy for such a tender thing!

**Romeo**   Is love a tender thing? Surely it's too rough, too aggressive? It pricks like a thorn!

**Mercutio**   If love is rough with you, be rough with love! If it pricks, prick it back. It'll soon collapse! [*To a* **Torchbearer**] Give me a cover for my face – an ugly mask for an ugly mug! What do I care if an inquisitive eye notices my deformities? [*The* **Torchbearer** *hands him a mask with bright red cheeks and huge eyebrows*] Here are the beetle brows that will cover up my embarrassment! [*He puts it on*]

**Benvolio**   Come on, knock on the door and let's go in. Once inside, everyone must start dancing.

**Romeo**   Torch-bearing for me. I'll leave carpet-tickling to lighthearted revellers. An old-fashioned proverb fits me: 'The spectator sees most of the game.' The party is at its brightest now, and I feel done in.

**Mercutio**   'Dun's the mouse!' as the old constables used to say as they lay in wait. If you mean 'Dun-the-carthorse', we'll pull you out of the mud. Or – begging your pardon – out of *love*, in which you are stuck up to the ears. Come along, we're wasting daylight . . .

**Romeo**    Nay, that's not so.

**Mercutio**                              I mean sir, in delay
45    We waste our lights in vain, light lights by day.
    Take our good meaning, for our judgement sits
    Five times in that ere once in our five wits.

**Romeo**    And we mean well in going to this masque,
    But 'tis no wit to go.

**Mercutio**                              Why, may one ask?

**Romeo**    I dreamt a dream tonight.

50 **Mercutio**                              And so did I.

**Romeo**    Well, what was yours?

**Mercutio**                              That dreamers often lie.

**Romeo**    In bed asleep, while they do dream things true.

**Mercutio**    O then I see Queen Mab hath been with you.
    She is the fairies' midwife, and she comes
55    In shape no bigger than an agate stone
    On the forefinger of an alderman,
    Drawn with a team of little atomies
    Over men's noses as they lie asleep.
    Her chariot is an empty hazelnut
60    Made by the joiner squirrel or old grub,
    Time out o' mind the fairies' coachmakers;
    Her waggon-spokes made of long spinners' legs,
    The cover of the wings of grasshoppers,
    Her traces of the smallest spider web,
65    Her collars of the moonshine's watery beams,
    Her whip of cricket's bone, the lash of film,
    Her waggoner a small grey-coated gnat,
    Not half so big as a round little worm
    Pricked from the lazy finger of a maid;

**Romeo**   Now that's not so!

**Mercutio**   I mean, sir, that in delaying we are wasting our
torches in vain, like lighting lights in daytime. Always take the
meaning that's the obvious one. There's five times more
sense in that than in the clever alternatives.

**Romeo**   We mean well in going to this masque, but it isn't wise
to go.

**Mercutio**   Why, may one ask?

**Romeo**   I dreamt a dream last night.

**Mercutio**   So did I.

**Romeo**   Well, what was yours?

**Mercutio**   That dreamers often lie –

**Romeo**   – in bed asleep, while they dream things that are true.

**Mercutio**   Oh, then I see that Queen Mab has been with you!
She's the fairy who brings to life men's fantasies. She's no
bigger than an agate stone on the index finger of an alderman.
A group of tiny creatures draws her waggon over men's noses
as they lie asleep. Her chariot is an empty hazelnut, made by a
squirrel joiner or an old worm – from time immemorial the
fairies' coachmakers. The spokes of the waggon-wheels are
made of long spiders' legs; the canopy of the wings of
grasshoppers; the harnesses of the smallest spider's web; the
collars of thin shafts of moonlight on the water; her whip of
cricket's bone, the lash of gossamer. Her waggoner is a small,
grey-coated gnat, not half as big as a round little worm
removed with a needle from the finger of a lazy maiden. And

61

70 And in this state she gallops night by night
Through lovers' brains, and then they dream of love;
O'er courtiers' knees, that dream on curtsies straight;
O'er lawyers' fingers who straight dream on fees;
O'er ladies' lips, who straight on kisses dream,
75 Which oft the angry Mab with blisters plagues
Because their breaths with sweetmeats tainted are.
Sometimes she gallops o'er a courtier's nose
And then dreams he of smelling out a suit;
And sometime comes she with a tithe-pig's tail,
80 Tickling a parson's nose as a lies asleep;
Then dreams he of another benefice.
Sometime she driveth o'er a soldier's neck
And then dreams he of cutting foreign throats,
Of breaches, ambuscados, Spanish blades,
85 Of healths five fathom deep; and then anon
Drums in his ear, at which he starts and wakes,
And being thus frighted swears a prayer or two
And sleeps again. This is that very Mab
That plaits the manes of horses in the night
90 And bakes the elf-locks in foul sluttish hairs,
Which, once untangled, much misfortune bodes.
This the hag, when maids lie on their backs,
That presses them and learns them first to bear,
Making them women of good carriage.
This is she –

95 **Romeo**          Peace, peace, Mercutio, peace.
Thou talk'st of nothing.

**Mercutio**          True, I talk of dreams,
Which are the children of an idle brain,
Begot of nothing but vain fantasy,
Which is as thin of substance as the air
100 And more inconstant than the wind, who woos
Even now the frozen bosom of the north

in this manner she gallops night after night through lover's brains: then they dream of love. Over the knees of courtiers, who immediately dream of respectful bows; over the fingers of lawyers: who straightway dream of fees; over ladies' lips (which the angry Mab often plagues with blisters, because their breaths are tainted with perfumed sweets), so that they dream immediately of kisses. Sometimes she gallops over a courtier's nose, and then he dreams he can smell out a commission. Sometimes she comes with the tail of a pig paid to the church in taxes, and with this she tickles a parson's nose as he lies asleep: then he dreams of a better parish. Sometimes she drives over a soldier's neck, whereupon he dreams of cutting enemy throats, of breakthroughs, ambushes, Spanish swords, drinking bouts; then she drums in his ear, making him start, and wake up. Being frightened like that, he swears a prayer or two, and goes back to sleep. This is the selfsame Mab who puts knots in the manes of horses during the night, and matts the hair of foul sluts. When the tangles are removed it forebodes misfortune. This is the hag who, when maids lie on their backs, presses on them, and teaches them how to bear children, making them 'women of good carriage'. This is she who –

**Romeo**   Hush, hush, Mercutio, quiet! You are talking a lot of nothing!

**Mercutio**   True. I'm talking about dreams, which are the offspring of a lazy brain. They're conceived by nothing but idle fantasy, which is as insubstantial as the air, and more unpredictable than the wind, which one moment favours the frozen north and then, becoming angry, blows away, turning

And, being angered, puffs away from thence
Turning his face to the dew-dropping south.

**Benvolio**    This wind you talk of blows us from ourselves:
105     Supper is done and we shall come too late.

**Romeo**    I fear too early for my mind misgives
Some consequence yet hanging in the stars
Shall bitterly begin his fearful date
With this night's revels, and expire the term
110     Of a despised life closed in my breast
By some vile forfeit of untimely death.
But he that hath the steerage of my course
Direct my suit. On, lusty gentlemen.

**Benvolio**    Strike, drum.

                                                    [*Exeunt*]


# Scene 5

*Capulet's house. Enter the* **Masquers.** **Servants** *come forth with napkins*


**First Servant**    Where's Potpan that he helps not to take away?
He shift a trencher! He scrape a trencher!

**Second Servant**    When good manners shall lie all in one or two
men's hands, and they unwashed too, 'tis a foul thing.

5    **First Servant**    Away with the joint-stools, remove the court-
cupboard, look to the plate. Good thou, save me a piece of
marchpane, and as thou loves me, let the porter let in Susan
Grindstone and Nell [*Exit* **Second Servant**] [*Enter* **Anthony**
*and* **Potpan**] – Anthony, and Potpan!

to face the milder south.

**Benvolio**   The wind you are talking about deflects us from our plans. Supper's over, and we shall arrive too late.

**Romeo**   Too early, I fear. I have a premonition that something written in the stars, but not yet revealed, will begin its fatal course with tonight's celebrations, foreclosing on my worthless life by means of some evil forfeit: an early death. But God who steers my life will direct my course. Press on, gentlemen.

**Benvolio**   [*To a follower*] Begin, drummer!

[*They all leave together*]


# Scene 5

*Capulet's house.* **Romeo** *and the other young* **Revellers** *are observing the scene. Two* **Servants** *enter*


**First Servant**   Where's Potpan gone who should be clearing things away? [*Scornfully*] Catch him moving a dish! Catch him scraping a plate!

**Second Servant**   It's come to something when good behaviour is confined to one or two men's hands, and those unwashed, too!

**First Servant**   Pack the stools away! Remove the sideboard! Take care of the silverware! Be a good fellow, and save me a piece of marzipan. And do me a favour: tell the porter to let Susan Grindstone and Nell in. [*Exit* **Second Servant**] [*He shouts*] Antony and Potpan!

[**Antony** *and* **Potpan** *enter*]                65

10 **Anthony**   Ay boy, ready.

**First Servant**   You are looked for and called for, asked for and
sought for, in the great chamber.

**Potpan**   We cannot be here and there too. Cheerly, boys! Be
brisk awhile, and the longer liver take all.

[*Exeunt* **Servants**]

[*Enter* **Capulet, Lady Capulet, Juliet, Tybalt, Nurse** *and all
the* **Guests** *and* **Gentlewomen** *to the* **Masquers**]

15 **Capulet**   Welcome, gentlemen, ladies that have their toes
Unplagued with corns will have a bout with you.
Ah ha, my mistresses! Which of you all
Will now deny to dance? She that makes dainty,
She I'll swear hath corns. Am I come near ye now?
20 Welcome gentlemen. I have seen the day
That I have worn a visor and could tell
A whispering tale in a fair lady's ear,
Such as would please. 'Tis gone, 'tis gone, 'tis gone,
You are welcome, gentlemen: come, musicians, play.
25 A hall, a hall, give room! And foot it girls!

[*Music plays and they dance*]

More light, you knaves, and turn the tables up.
And quench the fire, the room is grown too hot.
Ah sirrah, this unlooked-for sport comes well.
Nay sit, nay sit, good cousin Capulet,
30 For you and I are past our dancing days.
How long is't now since last yourself and I
Were in a masque?

**Cousin Capulet**            By'r Lady, thirty years.

**Antony**   [*saluting*] Ay, lad! Ready!

**First Servant**   They're looking and calling for you, asking for you and seeking you, in the Great Hall!

**Potpan**   We can't be everywhere. Cheer up, lads! Enjoy yourselves while you can, and may he who lives longest take all.

[*The* **Servants** *leave*]

[*Enter* **Lord** *and* **Lady Capulet, Juliet, Tybalt, Nurse, Guests** *and* **Musicians**]

**Capulet**   [*Greeting the maskers*] Welcome, gentlemen! The ladies who don't suffer from corns will join you in a dance! [*The ladies don't look too happy about this*] Aha, ladies! Which of you declines the invitation? Anyone who looks shy – I'll swear she has corns! [*The ladies blush*] Ah – touché! [*To the maskers again*] Welcome, gentlemen. I've seen the day when I've worn a mask, and knew how to whisper sweet nothings into a beautiful girl's ear! But not now, not now, not now. [*He sighs in the happy memory*] You are welcome, gentlemen. Come musicians, play! Clear the floor! Make room! Off you go, girls!

[*The music and dancing starts*]

[*To the* **Servants**] More light, clots! Fold the tables away! Dowse the fire – the room is getting too hot. [*To himself*] Lucky these maskers turned up. [*To his* **Cousin**] Do sit down, good cousin Capulet. You and I are past our dancing days. How long would it be now since we wore masks?

**Cousin**   Bless me – thirty years!

**Capulet**   What, man, 'tis not so much, 'tis not so much.
'Tis since the nuptial of Lucentio,
35  Come Pentecost as quickly as it will,
Some five and twenty years: and then we masqued.

**Cousin Capulet**   'Tis more, 'tis more, his son is elder, sir:
His son is thirty.

**Capulet**                Will you tell me that?
His son was but a ward two years ago.

40  **Romeo**   What lady's that which doth enrich the hand
Of yonder knight?

**Servant**                I know not, sir.

**Romeo**   O, she doth teach the torches to burn bright.
It seems she hangs upon the cheek of night
As a rich jewel in an Ethiop's ear –
45  Beauty too rich for use, for earth too dear.
So shows a snowy dove trooping with crows
As yonder lady o'er her fellows shows.
The measure done, I'll watch her place of stand,
And touching hers, make blessed my rude hand.
50  Did my heart love till now? Forswear it, sight.
For I ne'er saw true beauty till this night.

**Tybalt**   This by his voice should be a Montague.
Fetch me my rapier, boy. What, dares the slave
Come hither, covered with an antic face
55  To fleer and scorn at our solemnity?
Now by the stock and honour of my kin,
To strike him dead I hold it not a sin.

**Capulet**   Why how now, kinsman, wherefore storm you so?

**Tybalt**   Uncle, this is a Montague, our foe:
60  A villain that is hither come in spite
To scorn at our solemnity this night.

**Capulet**   What, man? Not so long, not so long! It was at
Lucentio's wedding; come Whit Sunday, about twenty-five
years ago. We masked then!

**Cousin**   It's more. It's more. His son is older, sir. His son is thirty.

**Capulet**   I don't believe it! His son was only a child two years
ago.

**Romeo**   [*to a* **Servant**] Who's the lady who's gracing the hand
of that gentleman there? [*It is* **Juliet**]

**Servant**   I don't know, sir.

**Romeo**   [*to himself*] Oh, torches look dim beside her! She
embellishes night like a rich jewel in an Ethiopian's ear – too
beautiful for everyday use, too valuable for this world. She
stands out like a snow-white dove amongst the crows. Once
the dance is over, I'll see where she stands, and make my
rough hand blessed by touching hers. Did my heart know real
love till now? My eyes need look no further: I hadn't see true
beauty till tonight.

**Tybalt**   [*overhearing*] This must be a Montague, judging by his
voice. [*To his page*] Fetch me my rapier, boy. [*The page
leaves*] How dare the wretch come here wearing a zany face,
to jeer and mock at our festivities? By my family's ancestors
and honour – I'd regard it no sin to strike him dead!

**Capulet**   [*passing by and noticing* **Tybalt**'s *anger*] Hello, there,
kinsman! What's annoying you so much?

**Tybalt**   Uncle, this is a Montague, one of our foes: a villain
who's come here in hatred, to mock at our celebration tonight!

**Capulet**    Young Romeo is it?

**Tybalt**                                    'Tis he, that villain Romeo.

**Capulet**    Content thee, gentle coz, let him alone,
    A bears him like a portly gentleman;
65   And, to say truth, Verona brags of him
    To be a virtuous and well-governed youth.
    I would not for the wealth of all this town
    Here in my house do him disparagement.
    Therefore, be patient, take no note of him.
70   It is my will, the which if thou respect,
    Show a fair presence and put off these frowns,
    An ill-beseeming semblance for a feast.

**Tybalt**    It fits when such a villain is a guest:
    I'll not endure him.

**Capulet**                                    He shall be endured.
75   What, goodman boy! I say he shall! Go to,
    Am I the master here or you? Go to.
    You'll not endure him! God shall mend my soul,
    You'll make a mutiny among my guests,
    You will set cock-a-hoop, you'll be the man!

**Tybalt**    Why, uncle, 'tis a shame.

80 **Capulet**                                    Go to, go to.
    You are a saucy boy. Is't so indeed?
    This trick may chance to scathe you, I know what.
    You must contrary me. Marry, 'tis time –
    Well said, my hearts – You are a princox, go
85   Be quiet, or – More light! More light! – For shame,
    I'll make you quiet. What, cheerly, my hearts!

**Tybalt**    Patience perforce with wilful choler meeting
    Makes my flesh tremble in their different greeting.

**Capulet**  Young Romeo, is it?

**Tybalt**  That's him! That villain, Romeo!

**Capulet**  Calm yourself, dear boy; leave him alone. He's behaving like a civilized gentleman. Frankly, Verona is justly proud of him as a virtuous and well-behaved youth. Not for all the wealth in the city would I be impolite to him here in my house. So be patient. Take no notice of him. That's my decision: if you respect it, behave in a friendly way, and stop frowning, it's quite inappropriate for a feast.

**Tybalt**  It's right when such a villain is a guest. I'll not tolerate him!

**Capulet**  He *is* to be tolerated! What, young Mister Nobody? I say he shall! [*Indignant*] Well, really! Am I the master here, or you? Really! [*Mocking*] You'll not endure him! God bless my soul, you'll start a rumpus amongst my guests? You'll throw your weight about? You'll play the man?

**Tybalt**  Why, uncle, it's shameful!

**Capulet**  Really, really! You're a cheeky fellow. So it's shameful is it? This will do you no good, mark my words. You'll go against me? Well, it's time – [*He breaks off to acknowledge the dancers*] Well said, dear friends! [*Back to* **Tybalt**] You're a cocky young pup. Either go, be quiet, or – [*To* **Servants**] More lights! More lights! [*To* **Tybalt**] For shame! I'll quieten you down. [*To the dancers*] Bravo, dear friends!

[*He turns away and circulates amongst the company*]

**Tybalt**  Having to control myself when he's so unreasonably angry has got my nerves on edge. I'll go. This Montague

I will withdraw; but this intrusion shall
90    Now seeming sweet, convert to bitterest gall.

[*Exit*]

**Romeo**    If I profane with my unworthiest hand
This holy shrine, the gentle sin is this:
My lips, two blushing pilgrims, ready stand
To smooth that rough touch with a tender kiss.

95    **Juliet**    Good pilgrim, you do wrong your hand too much,
Which mannerly devotion shows in this;
For saints have hands that pilgrims' hands do touch,
And palm to palm is holy palmers' kiss.

**Romeo**    Have not saints lips, and holy palmers too?

100    **Juliet**    Ay, pilgrim, lips that they must use in prayer.

**Romeo**    O then, dear saint, let lips do what hands do!
They pray. Grant thou, lest faith turn to despair.

**Juliet**    Saints do not move, though grant for prayer's sake.

**Romeo**    Then move not, while my prayer's effect I take.
105    Thus from my lips, by thine, my sin is purged.

**Juliet**    Then have my lips the sin that they have took.

**Romeo**    Sin from my lips? O trespass sweetly urged!
Give me my sin again.

**Juliet**                    You kiss by the book.

**Nurse**    Madam, your mother craves a word with you.

**Romeo**    What is her mother?

110    **Nurse**                    Marry, bachelor,
Her mother is the lady of the house,
And a good lady, and a wise and virtuous.

intrusion may be welcome now, but later it will turn bitterly sour!

[*He goes*]

**Romeo**   [*Taking* **Juliet** *by the hand*] If I'm profaning a holy shrine with my most unworthy hand, the lesser sin is this: my lips, like two blushing pilgrims, are ready with a tender kiss to smooth away the roughness of my touch.

**Juliet**   Dear pilgrim, you wrong your hand too much. It is only showing true devotion. Statues of saints are touched by pilgrims' hands, so placing palm-on-palm is a holy pilgrim's kiss.

**Romeo**   Don't saints have lips, and holy pilgrims too?

**Juliet**   Oh yes, pilgrim. Lips that they must use for prayer.

**Romeo**   Well then, dear saint, let lips do what hands do. Their prayer is: 'Grant a kiss, in case I lose my faith.'

**Juliet**   Saints grant prayers, but they don't move.

**Romeo**   Then stay still, while my prayer is granted.

[*He kisses her;* **Juliet** *is statuesque*]

Now the sin of my lips is purged by yours.

**Juliet**   So my lips must have the sin they've taken from you.

**Romeo**   Taken sin from my lips? You've sweetly proved that I've offended! Give me my sin back again! [*He kisses her for the second time*]

**Juliet**   You kiss very formally!

**Nurse**   Madam, your mother would like a word with you. [**Juliet** *leaves*]

**Romeo**   Who is her mother?

**Nurse**   Indeed, young gentleman, her mother is the lady of the house. She's a good, wise and virtuous lady. I nursed her

I nursed her daughter that you talked withal.
I tell you, he that can lay hold of her
Shall have the chinks.

115 **Romeo**                    Is she a Capulet?
O dear account! My life is my foe's debt.

**Benvolio**   Away, be gone; the sport is at the best.

**Romeo**   Ay, so I fear; the more is my unrest.

**Capulet**   Nay, gentlemen, prepare not to be gone,
120   We have a trifling foolish banquet towards.
Is it e'en so? Why then, I thank you all;
I thank you honest gentlemen, good night.
More torches here. Come on then, let's to bed.
Ah, sirrah, by my fay, it waxes late.
125   I'll to my rest.

                              [*Exeunt all but* **Juliet** *and* **Nurse**]

**Juliet**   Come hither Nurse. What is yond gentleman?

**Nurse**   The son and heir of old Tiberio.

**Juliet**   What's he that now is going out of door?

**Nurse**   Marry, that I think be young Petruchio.

130 **Juliet**   What's he that follows here, that would not dance?

**Nurse**   I know not.

**Juliet**   Go ask his name. If he be married,
My grave is like to be my wedding bed.

**Nurse**   His name is Romeo, and a Montague,
The only son of your great enemy.

135 **Juliet**   My only love sprung from my only hate.
Too early seen unknown, and known too late.

daughter that you've just been talking to. I tell you, the man who gets her will be in the money!

**Romeo**  Is she a Capulet? [*His face falls*] That's bad news! Now I'm pledged to my enemy!

**Benvolio**  [*catching him by the arm*] Let's go. We've had the best of the party.

**Romeo**  [*still stunned by the* **Nurse's** *revelation*] So I fear; much to my distress.

**Capulet**  [*politely encouraging the* **Maskers** *to stay longer*] Nay, gentlemen, don't go yet. We'll be having some simple refreshments shortly. [*The* **Maskers** *whisper their excuses to him*] Really? Well, then, my thanks to you all. Thanks, gentlemen. Good night! [*To the* **Servants**] Some more lights here! Come on then: let's go to bed. [*He yawns*] Upon my word, it's getting late. I'm off to bed.

[*Everyone goes except* **Juliet** *and the* **Nurse**]

**Juliet**  Come here, Nurse. [*Nodding towards a guest*] Who's the gentleman over there?

**Nurse**  Old Tiberio's son and heir.

**Juliet**  Who's that just leaving?

**Nurse**  I think that must be young Petruchio.

**Juliet**  [*getting to the real point at last*] Who's the one following behind the others, who wouldn't dance?

**Nurse**  I don't know.

**Juliet**  Go and ask his name. [*the* **Nurse** *leaves*] If he's already married, the only wedding-bed I'll ever have will be my grave!

**Nurse**  [*returning*] His name's Romeo, and he's a Montague. He's the only son of your great enemy.

**Juliet**  [*to herself*] The one I love the son of the one I hate! When I first met him, unrecognized. Now – too late – I know who he

Prodigious birth of love it is to me
That I must love a loathed enemy.

140    **Nurse**    What's this? What's this?

**Juliet**                            A rhyme I learned even now
Of one I danced withal.

[*One calls within 'Juliet!'*]

**Nurse**                      Anon, anon!
Come, let's away. The strangers are all gone.

[*Exeunt*]

is! How disastrous that first love for me should be a hated enemy!

**Nurse**    [*overhearing*] What's this? What's this?

**Juliet**    [*hastily*] Just a rhyme I learned from someone I danced with.

[**Juliet's** *mother calls her*]

**Nurse**    Coming! Coming! Let's be off. The visitors have all gone.

[*They leave*]

# Act two

## The Prologue

[*Enter* **Chorus**]

**Chorus**  Now old desire doth in his deathbed lie
And young affection gapes to be his heir;
That fair for which love groaned for and would die,
With tender Juliet matched, is now not fair.
5  Now Romeo is beloved, and loves again,
Alike bewitched by the charm of looks;
But to his foe supposed he must complain,
And she steal love's sweet bait from fearful hooks.
Being held a foe, he may not have access
10  To breathe such vows as lovers use to swear;
And she as much in love, her means much less
To meet her new beloved any where.
But passion lends them power, time means, to meet,
Tempering extremities with extreme sweet.

[*Exit*]

## Scene 1

*A lane by the wall of Capulet's orchard. Enter* **Romeo**

**Romeo**  Can I go forward when my heart is here?
Turn back, dull earth, and find thy centre out.

# Act two

## Prologue

*The* **Announcer** *returns to the stage*

**Announcer**   The old love-affair is dead now, and a new love
yearns to take its place. The beautiful Rosaline, once so
desirable and worth dying for, is now not beautiful when
compared with lovely Juliet. Now, Romeo is loved, and he
loves again. Both he and Juliet are bewitched by the magic
spell of loving looks. He must court a so-called enemy.
Responding, she must take some mortal risks. Being a foe, he
can't see her to swear the usual lovers' vows. And she, just as
much in love, has even fewer opportunities to meet her newly-
beloved, anywhere. Passion gives them a motive, and time
the means, to meet: their hardships make encounters all the
sweeter.

## Scene 1

*A street at the side of Capulet's house.* **Romeo** *enters, walking
homewards. He stops after a few paces*

**Romeo**   Can I go on further, when my heart is here? I must turn
back, mere mortal that I am, and find the centre of my

[*Enter* **Benvolio** *and* **Mercutio**]

**Benvolio**    Romeo! My cousin, Romeo! Romeo!

**Mercutio**                                                    He is wise,
And, on my life, hath stolen him home to bed.

5   **Benvolio**    He ran this way, and leapt this orchard wall.
Call, good Mercutio.

**Mercutio**                    Nay, I'll conjure too.
Romeo! Humours! Madman! Passion! Lover!
Appear thou in the likeness of a sigh,
Speak but one rhyme and I am satisfied.
10   Cry but 'Ay, me!' Pronounce but 'love' and 'dove',
Speak to my gossip Venus one fair word,
One nickname for her purblind son and heir,
Young Abraham Cupid, he that shot so trim
When King Cophetua loved the beggar maid.
15   He heareth not, he stirreth not, he moveth not;
The ape is dead, and I must conjure him.
I conjure thee by Rosaline's bright eyes,
By her high forehead and her scarlet lip.
By her fine foot, straight leg, and quivering thigh,
20   And the demesnes that there adjacent lie,
That in thy likeness thou appear to us.

**Benvolio**    And if he hear thee, thou wilt anger him.

**Mercutio**    This cannot anger him. 'Twould anger him
To raise a spirit in his mistress' circle
25   Of some strange nature, letting it there stand
Till she had laid it and conjured it down;
That were some spite. My invocation
Is fair and honest: in his mistress' name
I conjure only but to raise up him.

universe. [*He climbs over* **Juliet**'s *garden wall*]

[**Benvolio** *and* **Mercutio** *enter, looking for their lost companion*]

**Benvolio**    [*calling*] Romeo! Cousin Romeo! Romeo!

**Mercutio**    He's got sense! I do believe he's slipped off home to bed!

**Benvolio**    He ran this way, and jumped over this orchard wall. Call him, Mercutio.

**Mercutio**    I'll say the magic words. [*Calling*] Romeo! Moody-blue! Madman! Passion-flower! Heartache! [*Pretending to be a magician summoning spirits*] Materialize in the form of a lover's sigh, speak just one line of poetry and I'll be satisfied. Just cry 'Ah, me!' Rhyme 'love' and 'dove'! Speak one kind word to dear old Venus! Give her son and heir, the stone-blind ageless Cupid, – the one who made King Cophetua fall in love with the beggar-maid – a nickname! [*He puts his hand to his ear, listening for a reply*] Romeo neither hears, nor stirs, nor moves. The fool is dead. I'll have to summon him back again. [*He draws a circle on the ground with his sword, like a sorcerer at work on a spell*] I call on you in the name of Rosaline's bright eyes – by her beautiful forehead and her scarlet lips – by her fine feet, shapely legs and quivering thighs (and all the adjacent areas) – to rise and appear to us in the flesh!

**Benvolio**    [*suppressing his laughter*] If he hears you, he'll be furious!

**Mercutio**    Not at all! He'd be more angry if I called up a spirit to rise up inside the circle of his loved one! Then let it stand there till she exorcised it, and made it shrink away! That *would* be annoying! My spell is fair and honest: I call on the spirits in the name of his loved-one, purely to stiffen his resolve.

30 **Benvolio**   Come, he hath hid himself among these trees
    To be consorted with the humorous night.
    Blind is his love, and best befits the dark.

**Mercutio**   If love be blind, love cannot hit the mark.
    Now will he sit under a medlar tree
35 And wish his mistress were that kind of fruit
    As maids call medlars when they laugh alone.
    O Romeo, that she were, O that she were
    An open-arse and thou a poperin pear!
    Romeo, good night. I'll to my truckle-bed.
40 This field-bed is too cold for me to sleep.
    Come, shall we go?

**Benvolio**                Go then, for 'tis vain
    To seek him here that means not to be found.

[*Exeunt* **Benvolio** *and* **Mercutio**]


## Scene 2

*Capulet's orchard. Enter* **Romeo**


**Romeo**   He jests at scars that never felt a wound.

[*Enter* **Juliet** *above*]

    But soft, what light through yonder window breaks?
    It is the east and Juliet is the sun!
    Arise fair sun and kill the envious moon
5 Who is already sick and pale with grief
    That thou her maid art far more fair than she.
    Be not her maid since she is envious,

**Benvolio**    [*pulling* **Mercutio** *away*] Come on. He's hidden himself amongst the trees, to commune with the mysteries of night. His love is blind. It's best suited to the dark.

**Mercutio**    If love is blind, love cannot find its way. Now Romeo will sit beneath a medlar tree, wishing his girl friend was a medlar fruit, which girls make secret jokes about because they look so sexy. O, Romeo! Would that she were, if only she were, what yokels call the medlar – an 'open arse', with you a pop-it-in pear! [*He blows a kiss*] Romeo, good night! I'm off to my little cot. This sleeping out of doors is too cold for me. Come on – shall we go?

**Benvolio**    Yes indeed. It's pointless looking for someone who's determined not to be found.

[*They leave*]

## Scene 2

*Capulet's garden.* **Romeo** *has heard all* **Mercutio**'s *bawdy remarks*

**Romeo**    Mercutio mocks love's scars: he has never been wounded. [*He sees* **Juliet** *at the window of Capulet's house*] But hush! Is that a light shining through the window there? It's like the east, with Juliet the sun. Rise up, fair sun, and kill the jealous moon! It looks sick already, and pale with grief because you're far lovelier than she is, though only her servant. Since she's jealous, quit her service! Her uniform is a

       Her vestal livery is but sick and green
       And none but fools do wear it. Cast it off.
10    It is my lady, O it is my love!
       O that she knew she were!
       She speaks, yet she says nothing. What of that?
       Her eye discourses, I will answer it.
       I am too bold. 'Tis not to me she speaks.
15    Two of the fairest stars in all the heaven,
       Having some business, do entreat her eyes
       To twinkle in their spheres till they return.
       What if her eyes were there, they in her head?
       The brightness of her cheek would shame those stars
20    As daylight doth a lamp. Her eyes in heaven
       Would through the airy region stream so bright
       That birds would sing and think it were not night.
       See how she leans her cheek upon her hand.
       O that I were a glove upon that hand,
       That I might touch that cheek!

**Juliet**                      Ay me!

25 **Romeo**                 She speaks.
       O speak again bright angel, for thou art
       As glorious to this night, being o'er my head,
       As is a winged messenger of heaven
       Unto the white-upturned wondering eyes
30    Of mortals that fall back to gaze on him
       When he bestrides the lazy-pacing clouds
       And sails upon the bosom of the air.

**Juliet**   O Romeo, Romeo, wherefore art thou Romeo?
       Deny thy father and refuse thy name.
35    And I'll no longer be a Capulet.

**Romeo**   Shall I hear more, or shall I speak at this?

**Juliet**   'Tis but thy name that is my enemy;
       Thou art thyself, though not a Montague.

sickly green: only court jesters and virgins wear that. Cast it off! [**Juliet** *walks on to the balcony*] It is my lady-love! If only she knew it! Her lips move – but she says nothing. That doesn't matter: her eyes speak for her, and I'll answer them. [*He opens his mouth to address her, but his courage fails*] I'm too forward. She isn't speaking to me. Two of the most beautiful stars in all the sky have asked her eyes to take their place while they go off on business somewhere! And what if they have changed places? The brightness of her cheeks would put those stars to shame, as daylight does a lamp. Her eyes, sparkling so brightly in heaven, would make birds sing, because they'd think that day had dawned. Look how she leans her cheek upon her hand! Oh, if only I were a glove upon that hand, so I could touch that cheek!

**Juliet**  [*sighing heavily*] Oh, dear!

**Romeo**  She speaks. Oh, speak again, bright angel! Being up above me, you enhance this night, like an angel seen by astonished mortals, who gaze aloft in wide-eyed amazement as he sits astride a slow-moving cloud, and sails upon the sustaining air!

**Juliet**  Oh, Romeo, Romeo! Why must you be Romeo? Renounce your father and reject your name. Or, if you won't, just swear your love to me, and I'll no longer be a Capulet.

**Romeo**  [*to himself*] Shall I hear some more, or speak now?

**Juliet**  It's only your name that's my enemy. You'd be the same, even if you weren't a Montague. What's 'Montague'? It's not a

What's Montague? It is nor hand nor foot
40  Nor arm nor face nor any other part
Belonging to a man. O be some other name.
What's in a name? That which we call a rose
By any other word would smell as sweet.
So Romeo would, were he not Romeo called,
45  Retain that dear perfection which he owes
Without that title. Romeo, doff thy name,
And for that name, which is no part of thee,
Take all myself.

**Romeo**              I take thee at thy word.
Call me but love, and I'll be new baptised:
50  Henceforth I never will be Romeo.

**Juliet**   What man art thou that thus bescreened in night
So stumblest on my counsel?

**Romeo**                        By a name
I know not how to tell thee who I am:
My name, dear saint, is hateful to myself
55  Because it is an enemy to thee.
Had I it written, I would tear the word.

**Juliet**   My ears have yet not drunk a hundred words
Of thy tongue's uttering, yet I know the sound.
Art thou not Romeo, and a Montague?

60  **Romeo**   Neither, fair maid, if either thee dislike.

**Juliet**   How cam'st thou hither, tell me, and wherefore?
The orchard walls are high and hard to climb,
And the place death, considering who thou art,
If any of my kinsmen find thee here.

65  **Romeo**   With love's light wings did I o'erperch these walls,
For stony limits cannot hold love out,
And what love can do, that dares love attempt:
Therefore thy kinsmen are no stop to me.

hand, or a foot, or an arm, or a face, or any other part of a man's anatomy. Take some other name! What's so significant about a name? What we call a rose would smell as sweet, whatever word we used for it. If Romeo wasn't called Romeo, he'd still retain his own dear perfection without his name. Romeo – give up your name and in exchange for that name, which is not part of you, take all of me!

**Romeo**   [*to* **Juliet** *now*] I'll take you at your word. Baptize me again, and I'll take the name of 'Love'. From now on, I've finished with 'Romeo'.

**Juliet**   [*startled*] Who is there, hidden in the darkness, overhearing my private thoughts?

**Romeo**   I don't like to use my name to tell you who I am. My name, dear saint, is hateful to me because it's an enemy of yours. If it was written, I'd tear it up.

**Juliet**   I haven't heard you speak a hundred words, but I recognize your voice. Are you not Romeo, and a Montague?

**Romeo**   Neither, fair maid, if either displeases you.

**Juliet**   Tell me, how did you get here, and why? The walls of the orchard are high and hard to climb. Considering who you are, this place is death to you if any of my relatives find you here.

**Romeo**   I flew over these walls on the light wings of love. Stone boundaries can't keep love out. Love dares to do what love can. Therefore your relatives are no barrier to me.

**Juliet**   If they do see thee, they will murder thee.

70 **Romeo**   Alack, there lies more peril in thine eye
Than twenty of their swords. Look thou but sweet
And I am proof against their enmity.

**Juliet**   I would not for the world they saw thee here.

**Romeo**   I have night's cloak to hide me from their eyes,
75 And but thou love me, let them find me here.
My life were better ended by their hate
Than death prorogued, wanting of thy love.

**Juliet**   By whose direction found'st thou out this place?

**Romeo**   By love, that first did prompt me to enquire.
80 He lent me counsel, and I lent him eyes.
I am no pilot, yet wert thou as far
As that vast shore washed with the farthest sea,
I should adventure for such merchandise.

**Juliet**   Thou knowest the mask of night is on my face,
85 Else would a maiden blush bepaint my cheek
For that which thou hast heard me speak tonight.
Fain would I dwell on form; fain, fain deny
What I have spoke. But farewell compliment!
Dost thou love me? I know thou wilt say 'Ay',
90 And I will take thy word. Yet, if thou swearest,
Thou mayst prove false. At lovers' perjuries,
They say, Jove laughs. O gentle Romeo,
If thou dost love, pronounce it faithfully.
Or, if thou think'st I am too quickly won,
95 I'll frown and be perverse and say thee nay,
So thou wilt woo; but else, not for the world.
In truth, fair Montague, I am too fond,
And therefore thou mayst think my haviour light,
But trust me, gentleman, I'll prove more true
100 Than those that have more cunning to be strange.

**Juliet**  If they see you, they'll kill you.

**Romeo**  Alas, I'm more afraid of your eyes than twenty of their swords. Look fondly on me, and their enmity can do me no harm.

**Juliet**  Not for all the world would I have them see you here.

**Romeo**  The night conceals me from them. And provided you love me, let them find me here. I'd rather my life ended by their hate than I live on without your love.

**Juliet**  Who told you where to find me?

**Romeo**  Love did, which first prompted me to ask. He gave me advice, and I gave him my eyes to see with. I'm no pilot, but even if you were as far away as the farthest shore of the most distant sea, I'd set out in search of such a prize as you.

**Juliet**  You know night conceals my face; otherwise there'd be a maidenly blush colouring my cheeks, because of what you've heard me say tonight. I'd like to proceed in the conventional fashion: gladly, gladly deny what I've said – but farewell, etiquette! Do you love me? I know you'll say 'Yes', and I'll take your word for it. Because if you swear, you might default: they say Jove, the god of oaths, laughs at lover's promises because they're never kept. Oh, gentle Romeo, if you really do love me, say so in good faith. Or, if you think I'm yours too quickly – I'll frown, and be awkward, and say no to you, provided you'll keep wooing me. Otherwise, I wouldn't do it for all the world. Truly, dear Montague, I'm too loving, and therefore you may think I'm behaving immodestly. But trust me, sir. I'll prove more faithful than those pretending to be hard to get. I would have been more distant, I'll admit, but

I should have been more strange, I must confess,
But that thou overheard'st, ere I was ware,
My true love's passion. Therefore pardon me,
And not impute this yielding to light love,
105  Which the dark night hath so discovered.

**Romeo**    Lady, by yonder blessed moon I vow,
That tips with silver all these fruit-tree tops –

**Juliet**    O swear not by the moon, th' inconstant moon,
That monthly changes in her circled orb,
110  Lest that thy love prove likewise variable.

**Romeo**    What shall I swear by?

**Juliet**                              Do not swear at all;
Or, if thou wilt, swear by thy gracious self,
Which is the god of my idolatry,
And I'll believe thee.

**Romeo**                              If my heart's dear love –

115  **Juliet**    Well, do not swear. Although I joy in thee,
I have no joy of this contract tonight:
It is too rash, too unadvised, too sudden,
Too like the lightning, which doth cease to be
Ere one can say 'It lightens'. Sweet, good night.
120  This bud of love, by summer's ripening breath,
May prove a beauteous flower when next we meet.
Good night, and good night! As sweet repose and rest
Come to thy heart as that within my breast!

**Romeo**    O wilt thou leave me so unsatisfied?

125  **Juliet**    What satisfaction canst thou have tonight?

**Romeo**    The exchange of thy love's faithful vow for mine.

**Juliet**    I gave thee mine before thou didst request it,
And yet I would it were to give again.

you overheard my confession of love. Forgive me, therefore, and don't attribute this quick surrender – which night's darkness has revealed – to the lightness of my love.

**Romeo**    Lady, I vow by the blessed moon that puts a silver lining round the tops of those fruit trees –

**Juliet**    [*interrupting quickly*] Oh, don't swear by the moon – the changeable moon, that alters throughout its monthly course! – in case your love proves just as variable.

**Romeo**    What shall I swear by?

**Juliet**    Don't swear at all. Or, if you must, swear by your gracious self, which is the god I worship. Then I'll believe you.

**Romeo**    If my darling –

**Juliet**    So don't swear. Although I rejoice in your love, I take no joy from tonight's avowal. It is too rash. Too ill-advised. Too sudden. Too like lightning, which is over before one can say 'It lightens' Good night, sweetheart. When we next meet, this bud which is our love may have ripened into a beautiful flower. Goodnight, goodnight. May you sleep as sweet and soundly as I will.

**Romeo**    Oh, will you leave me so unsatisfied?

**Juliet**    What satisfaction is possible tonight?

**Romeo**    The exchange of our faithful vows.

**Juliet**    You had mine before you asked for it. Yet I wish I had it back, to give away again.

**Romeo**    Wouldst thou withdraw it? For what purpose, love?

130 **Juliet**    But to be frank and give it thee again;
        And yet I wish but for the thing I have.
        My bounty is as boundless as the sea,
        My love as deep; the more I give to thee
        The more I have, for both are infinite.
135    I hear some noise within. Dear love, adieu.

[**Nurse** *calls within*]

Anon, good Nurse! Sweet Montague be true.
Stay but a little, I will come again.

[*Exit* **Juliet**]

**Romeo**    O blessed, blessed night. I am afeard,
        Being in night, all this is but a dream,
140    Too flattering sweet to be substantial.

[*Enter* **Juliet** *above*]

**Juliet**    Three words, dear Romeo, and good night indeed.
        If that thy bent of love be honourable,
        Thy purpose marriage, send me word tomorrow
        By one that I'll procure to come to thee,
145    Where and what time thou wilt perform the rite,
        And all my fortunes at thy foot I'll lay,
        And follow thee my lord throughout the world.

**Nurse**    [*within*] Madam!

**Juliet**    I come, anon – But if thou meanest not well
        I do beseech thee –

**Nurse**    [*within*]        Madam!

**Romeo**   You'd like to withdraw it? Why, my love?

**Juliet**   Only to be prodigal, and give it you again. But I'm asking for what I already have. My generosity is as boundless as the sea. My love's as deep. The more I give you, the more I have. Both are infinite.

[*The **Nurse** calls*]

Someone's calling. Dear love, goodbye. [*To the **Nurse***] Coming, good Nurse! [*To **Romeo***] Sweet Montague, be faithful. Stay a moment. I'll be back.

[**Juliet** *leaves*]

**Romeo**   Oh, blessed, blessed night! Being night, I'm afraid all this is only a dream. It's too wonderful to be true.

[**Juliet** *comes out on the balcony above*]

**Juliet**   Just three more words, dear Romeo, and then it really is goodnight. If your intentions are honourable, and your object is marriage, send me word tomorrow (I'll arrange a messenger) where and when you'll go through the ceremony. My life will then be yours: I'll follow you, my lord, throughout the world.

**Nurse**   [*insistent*] Madam!

**Juliet**   [*over her shoulder*] Coming now! [*To **Romeo***] But if you aren't serious, I beg you –

**Nurse**   [*louder still*] Madam!

**Juliet**                              By and by I come –
150   To cease thy strife and leave me to my grief.
Tomorrow will I send.

**Romeo**                      So thrive my soul –

**Juliet**    A thousand times good night.

[*Exit* **Juliet**]

**Romeo**    A thousand times the worse, to want thy light.
155   Love goes toward love as schoolboys from their books,
But love from love, toward school with heavy looks.

[*Enter* **Juliet** *above*]

**Juliet**    Hist! Romeo, hist! O for a falconer's voice
To lure this tassel-gentle back again.
Bondage is hoarse and may not speak aloud,
160   Else would I tear the cave where Echo lies
And make her airy tongue more hoarse than mine
With repetition of my 'Romeo'.

**Romeo**    It is my soul that calls upon my name.
How silver-sweet sound lovers' tongues by night,
165   Like softest music to attending ears.

**Juliet**    Romeo!

**Romeo**              My dear?

**Juliet**                      What o'clock tomorrow
Shall I send to thee?

**Romeo**                      By the hour of nine.

**Juliet**    I will not fail. 'Tis twenty year till then.
I have forgot why I did call thee back.

170   **Romeo**    Let me stand here till thou remember it.

**Juliet**   Right now! [*To* **Romeo** *again*] – to court me no more, and leave me to my grief. I'll get in touch tomorrow.

**Romeo**   May my soul –

**Juliet**   [*interrupting in her haste*] A thousand times, goodnight! [*she goes in*]

**Romeo**   It's a thousand times less good, now your radiance has gone! Lovers seek their loved ones as schoolboys quit their books; lovers travel homewards like scholars trudging to school.

[**Romeo** *reluctantly turns away, but* **Juliet** *returns*]

**Juliet**   Pst! [*Calling*] Romeo! Pst! I wish I could recall him in the way a falconer retrieves his hawk! I daren't speak up in case my father hears. Otherwise, I'd make the goddess Echo hoarser than myself by shouting 'Romeo!' repeatedly in her cave!

**Romeo**   My soul is calling out my name. [*He turns*] Lovers' voices sound silvery-sweet at night, like music at its softest to the listening ear.

**Juliet**   Romeo.

**Romeo**   Dearest?

**Juliet**   What time tomorrow shall I send to you?

**Romeo**   By nine.

**Juliet**   I won't fail. It's twenty years till then. [*Pause*] I've forgotten why I called you back . . .

**Romeo**   Let me stand here till you remember.

**Juliet**    I shall forget, to have thee still stand there,
Remembering how I love thy company.

**Romeo**    And I'll still stay, to have thee still forget,
Forgetting any other home but this.

175 **Juliet**    'Tis almost morning. I would have thee gone;
And yet no farther than a wanton's bird,
That lets it hop a little from her hand,
Like a poor prisoner in his twisted gyves,
And with a silk thread plucks it back again,
180    So loving-jealous of his liberty.

**Romeo**    I would I were thy bird.

**Juliet**                              Sweet, so would I.
Yet I should kill thee with much cherishing.
Good night, good night! Parting is such sweet sorrow
That I shall say good night till it be morrow.

[*Exit*]

185 **Romeo**    Sleep dwell upon thine eyes, peace in thy breast!
Would I were sleep and peace, so sweet to rest!
Hence will I to my ghostly sire's close cell,
His help to crave and my dear hap to tell.

[*Exit*]

**Juliet**  I'll forget, just to keep you standing there: remembering only that I love your company.

**Romeo**  And I'll stay put just to keep you forgetful: forgetting that I've any home but this one.

**Juliet**  It's almost morning. I'd let you go now, but no further than a bird held by a playful girl. She'd let it hop a little from her hand, like a poor prisoner in fetters, then pluck it back with a silken thread, wanting to give it freedom, but too caring to part with it.

**Romeo**  I wish I were your bird!

**Juliet**  Sweet, so do I. But I'd kill you with too much kindness. Goodnight! Goodnight! Parting is such sweet sorrow: I could go on saying 'Goodnight' till morning.

[**Juliet** *leaves*]

**Romeo**  May sleep dwell upon your eyes, and peace in your breast! I wish I were 'sleep and peace', to rest so sweetly! I'll go now to my Father Confessor's private cell: to beg for his help and tell him my good fortune.

[*He goes*]

## Scene 3

*Friar Lawrence's cell. Enter* **Friar Lawrence** *with a basket*

**Friar Lawrence**    The gray-eyed morn smiles on the frowning
　　　night,
　　　Check'ring the eastern clouds with streaks of light;
　　　And fleckel'd darkness like a drunkard reels
5　　From forth day's path and Titan's fiery wheels.
　　　Now, ere the sun advance his burning eye
　　　The day to cheer and night's dank dew to dry,
　　　I must up-fill this osier cage of ours
　　　With baleful weeds and precious-juiced flowers.
10　The earth that's nature's mother is her tomb;
　　　What is her burying grave, that is her womb.
　　　And from her womb children of divers kind
　　　We sucking on her natural bosom find;
　　　Many for many virtues excellent,
15　None but for some, and yet all different.
　　　O, mickle is the powerful grace that lies
　　　In plants, herbs, stones, and their true qualities;
　　　For nought so vile that on the earth doth live
　　　But to the earth some special good doth give;
20　Nor aught so good but, strained from that fair use,
　　　Revolts from true birth, stumbling on abuse:
　　　Virtue itself turns vice, being misapplied,
　　　And vice sometime's by action dignified.
　　　Within the infant rind of this weak flower
25　Poison hath residence, and medicine power,
　　　For this, being smelt, with that part cheers each part;
　　　Being tasted, slays all senses with the heart.
　　　Two such opposed kings encamp them still
　　　In man as well as herbs – grace and rude will;
30　And where the worser is predominant,
　　　Full soon the canker death eats up that plant.

[*Enter* **Romeo**]

## Scene 3

**Friar Lawrence**'s *cell.* **Friar Lawrence** *enters, carrying a basket*

**Friar Lawrence**   The soft light of morning disperses sullen
night. Streaks of light stipple the eastern clouds. Mottled
darkness reels like a drunkard before the advancing sun.
Before the sun gets too hot, cheering the day and drying the
night's dew I must fill our basket with harmful weeds, and
flowers with precious juices. Earth is both nature's mother
and its grave. What dies is born again in great variety, and is
earth-nourished. Many plants have numerous fine qualities;
none is without some benefit, yet all are different. Great is the
medicinal power in plants, herbs, stones, and their essences.
There's nothing living on this earth so vile that it hasn't some
goodness to give – nor anything so good that it can't be
misused and abused. Misguided virtue can result in vice, and
vice can sometimes lead to a virtuous outcome.

[**Romeo** *enters, but does not make himself known yet.* **Friar
Lawrence** *chooses a sample from his collection*]

Within the seeds of this weak flower there is both poison and a
healing property. Smell it, and the whole body feels good.
Taste it, and one dies. It's the same with man as with herbs.
Goodness and evil, at war within, rule opposite camps. When
evil wins, the spirit dies.

[**Romeo** *comes forward and speaks*]

**Romeo**    Good morrow father!

**Friar Lawrence**                    Benedicite!
What early tongue so sweet saluteth me?
Young son, it argues a distempered head
35  So soon to bid good morrow to they bed.
Care keeps his watch in every old man's eye,
And where care lodges sleep will never lie;
But where unbruised youth with unstuffed brain
Doth couch his limbs, there golden sleep doth reign.
40  Therefore thy earliness doth me assure
Thou art uproused with some distemperature;
Or if not so, then here I hit it right –
Our Romeo hath not been in bed tonight.

**Romeo**    That last is true; the sweeter rest was mine.

45  **Friar Lawrence**    God pardon sin! Wast thou with Rosaline?

**Romeo**    With Rosaline, my ghostly father? No.
I have forgot that name, and that name's woe.

**Friar Lawrence**    That's my good son; but where hast thou
been then?

50  **Romeo**    I'll tell thee ere thou ask it me again.
I have been feasting with mine enemy,
Where, on a sudden, one hath wounded me
That's by me wounded. Both our remedies
Within thy help and holy physic lies.
55  I bear no hatred, blessed man, for lo,
My intercession likewise steads my foe.

**Friar Lawrence**    Be plain, good son, and homely in thy drift.
Riddling confession finds but riddling shrift.

**Romeo**    Then plainly know my heart's dear love is set
60  On the fair daughter of rich Capulet.
As mine on hers, so hers is set on mine;

**Romeo**    Good morning, Father.

**Friar Lawrence**    Bless you. [*He makes the sign of the cross*]
Who's greeting me so pleasantly, so early in the morning? My
son, to be up and out of bed so soon suggests a troubled mind.
Worry is an old man's problem: it causes sleeplessness. But
carefree young men sleep sweet with clear minds. To me,
your earliness means you're up because something is
bothering you. Or if not, I'm getting nearer – our Romeo hasn't
been to bed tonight!

**Romeo**    The last is true. I've enjoyed something better than
sleep.

**Friar Lawrence**    [*dismayed*] God forgive us! Have you been
with Rosaline?

**Romeo**    With Rosaline, Father? No. I've forgotten that name
and the suffering it caused me.

**Friar Lawrence**    [*relieved*] That's my good son. But where have
you been, then?

**Romeo**    I'll tell you to save you further questions. I've been to a
party at my enemy's, where suddenly someone wounded me,
and I wounded someone. With your help and holy powers,
you can make us both better. I bear no hatred, Father:
obviously, my request is equally to the advantage of this foe.

**Friar Lawrence**    [*patiently, not fully understanding*] Be simple,
good son, and speak out plainly. A riddle of a confession can
only result in a riddle of a penance.

**Romeo**    Not to mince words, I've set my heart on rich Capulet's
beautiful daughter. As I love her, she loves me: we are as one,

And all combined, save what thou must combine
By holy marriage. When, and where, and how,
We met, we wooed, and made exchange of vow,
65    I'll tell thee as we pass; but this I pray,
That thou consent to marry us today.

**Friar Lawrence**    Holy Saint Francis! What a change is here!
Is Rosaline, that thou didst love so dear,
So soon forsaken? Young men's love, then, lies
70    Not truly in their hearts, but in their eyes.
Jesu Maria, what a deal of brine
Hath washed thy sallow cheeks for Rosaline!
How much salt water thrown away in waste,
To season love, that of it doth not taste!
75    The sun not yet thy sighs from heaven clears,
Thy old groans yet ring in mine ancient ears;
Lo, here upon thy cheek the stain doth sit
Of an old tear that is not washed off yet.
If e'er thou wast thyself, and these woes thine,
80    Thou and these woes were all for Rosaline.
And art thou changed? Pronounce this sentence, then:
Women may fall, when there's no strength in men.

**Romeo**    Thou chid'st me oft for loving Rosaline.

**Friar Lawrence**    For doting, not for loving, pupil mine.

**Romeo**    And bad'st me bury love.

85 **Friar Lawrence**                                    Not in a grave
To lay one in, another out to have.

**Romeo**    I pray thee chide me not. Her I love now
Doth grace for grace and love for love allow;
The other did not so.

**Friar Lawrence**                        O, she knew well
90    Thy love did read by rote that could not spell.

except for what you must combine through holy marriage. When, and where, and how we met and wooed and exchanged vows I'll tell you as we stroll along. I beg of you only this: that you'll consent to marry us today.

**Friar Lawrence**  Holy Saint Francis! Now here's a change! Have you so soon forsaken Rosaline, whom you loved so dearly? Young men love with their eyes, then, not truly in their hearts! By Jesus and Mary, what oceans have washed your pale cheeks on behalf of Rosaline! How much salt water has been wasted to preserve love, and give it flavour, when it wasn't love at all! Your sighs still linger in the air. Your old groans still ring in my ancient ears. Look, there's a stain on your cheek of an old tear you haven't yet washed off! If you were genuine then, and felt those pangs, both were directed towards Rosaline. So you've changed? Consider the old saying: 'Women are unfaithful when men are weak.'

**Romeo**  You often told me off for loving Rosaline.

**Friar Lawrence**  For doting, not for *loving*, dear pupil.

**Romeo**  And you told me to bury my love!

**Friar Lawrence**  Not to put one into a grave, and take another one out.

**Romeo**  Please don't scold me. The one I love now returns my love. The other did not.

**Friar Lawrence**  Oh, she knew your love was like reciting before you'd learned to spell! But come on, young waverer, come

But come, young waverer, come go with me,
In one respect I'll thy assistant be;
For this alliance may so happy prove
To turn your households' rancour to pure love.

95 **Romeo**   O, let us hence; I stand on sudden haste.

**Friar Lawrence**   Wisely and slow; they stumble that run fast.

*[Exeunt]*

## Scene 4

*A street. Enter* **Benvolio** *and* **Mercutio**

**Mercutio**   Where the devil should this Romeo be?
Came he not home tonight?

**Benvolio**   Not to his father's. I spoke with his man.

**Mercutio**   Why, that same pale hard-hearted wench, that
5   Rosaline, torments him so that he will sure run mad.

**Benvolio**   Tybalt, the kinsman to old Capulet, hath sent a
letter to his father's house.

**Mercutio**   A challenge, on my life.

**Benvolio**   Romeo will answer it.

10 **Mercutio**   Any man that can write may answer a letter.

**Benvolio**   Nay, he will answer the letter's master, how he
dares, being dared.

along with me. There's one good reason why I'll assist you: this marriage could be the happy cause of turning the enmity between your two households into real love.

**Romeo**  Oh, let's go! The sooner the better!

**Friar Lawrence**  Wisely and slowly: those who run, trip.

[*They leave*]


# Scene 4

*A street.* **Mercutio** *and* **Benvolio** *are walking along*


**Mercutio**  Where the devil can this Romeo be? Didn't he come home last night?

**Benvolio**  Not to his father's. I asked his servant.

**Mercutio**  Why, that pale-faced, hard-hearted wench, that Rosaline, torments him to distraction!

**Benvolio**  Tybalt, Capulet's nephew, has sent a letter to Lord Montague's house.

**Mercutio**  A challenge, I'll be bound!

**Benvolio**  Romeo will answer it.

**Mercutio**  Anyone who can write can answer a letter.

**Benvolio**  I mean, he'll take up the challenge: show he's not scared, having been dared.

**Mercutio**    Alas, poor Romeo, he is already dead: stabbed with
a white wench's black eye; run through the ear with a love-
15    song; the very pin of his heart cleft with the blind bow-boy's
butt-shaft. And is he a man to encounter Tybalt?

**Benvolio**    Why, what is Tybalt?

**Mercutio**    More than Prince of Cats. O, he's the courageous
captain of compliments. He fights as you sing prick-song;
20    keeps time, distance, and proportion; he rest his minim rests,
one, two and the third in your bosom; the very butcher of a
silk button, a duellist, a duellist; a gentleman of the very first
house, of the first and second cause. Ah, the immortal
passado! The punto reverso! The hay –

25    **Benvolio**    The what?

**Mercutio**    The pox of such antic, lisping, affecting
fantasticoes; these new tuners of accent! 'By Jesu, a very good
blade! A very tall man! A very good whore!' Why, is not this a
lamentable thing, grandsire, that we should be thus afflicted
30    with these strange flies, these fashion-mongers, these pardon
me's, who stand so much on the new form that they cannot sit
at ease on the old bench? O, their bones, their bones!

[*Enter* **Romeo**]

**Benvolio**    Here comes Romeo, here comes Romeo.

**Mercutio**    Without his roe, like a dried herring. O flesh, flesh,
35    how art thou fishified! Now is he for the numbers that
Petrarch flowed in. Laura, to his lady, was a kitchen-wench –
marry, she had a better love to berhyme her; Dido, a dowdy;
Cleopatra, a gipsy; Helen and Hero, hildings and harlots;

**Mercutio**  Alas, poor Romeo! He's already dead: stabbed with a look from the dark eyes of that pale wench! Pierced through the ear by a love-song! The centre of his heart split by one of Cupid's practice shots! And he's going to fight with Tybalt?

**Benvolio**  Why, what's so great about Tybalt?

**Mercutio**  He's a Top Cat, only more so. He's like the Tybalt in our children's stories. Oh, he's very suave! He fights like you sing in close harmony, his timing, pace and rhythm are perfect. [*He demonstrates as he speaks, like a man fencing*] He pauses: one, two, then [*lunging forward*] stabs you in the bosom on the count of three! He can go through any shirt button he chooses: he's a duellist, a duellist, a top ranker, all according to fencing school rules. [**Mercutio** *demonstrates again*] Ah! His forward thrust! His back-hander! His [*his sword strikes home*] Hey!

**Benvolio**  His *what*!

**Mercutio**  Sod all such fancy, pansy, pretentious phoneys! These trendy talkers! [*He mocks an affected style of speech*] 'Jesus! An ace blade! He walks tall! Clever sonofabitch!' Why, isn't it deplorable, grandad, that we should have to put up with these foreign pests, these fashion plates, these [*an affected voice now*] 'ay-beg-your-ever-so-pardon-me's' who stand for all things new, so can't sit down on the old bench! [*He rubs his posterior and groans*] Oh, their bones! Their bones!

[**Romeo** *enters*]

**Benvolio**  Here's Romeo! Here's Romeo!

**Mercutio**  Without his 'Roe-saline', like a dried herring! Oh flesh, oh flesh! How fishified you are! Now he'll treat us to some passionate poetry. The poet Petrarch's Laura will be no more than a scullery-maid compared with his fair lady – but, mind you, Laura had a better poet rhyming for her! Dido will seem dowdy. Cleopatra a mere gypsy. Helen and Hero sluts

Thisbe, a gray eye or so, but not to the purpose. Signior
40　Romeo, bon jour! There's a French salutation to your French
slop. You gave us the counterfeit fairly last night.

**Romeo**　Good morrow to you both. What counterfeit did I give
you?

**Mercutio**　The slip, sir, the slip. Can you not conceive?

45　**Romeo**　Pardon, good Mercutio; my business was great, and
in such a case as mine a man may strain courtesy.

**Mercutio**　That's as much as to say, such a case as yours
constrains a man to bow in the hams.

**Romeo**　Meaning to curtsy.

50　**Mercutio**　Thou hast most kindly hit it.

**Romeo**　A most courteous exposition.

**Mercutio**　Nay, I am the very pink of courtesy.

**Romeo**　Pink for flower.

**Mercutio**　Right.

55　**Romeo**　Why, then is my pump well flowered.

**Mercutio**　Sure wit! Follow me this jest now till thou hast worn
out thy pump, that, when the single sole of it is worn, the jest
may remain, after the wearing, solely singular.

**Romeo**　O single-soled jest, solely singular for the singleness!

and whores. Thisbe not in the running, in spite of her grey eyes. [*He pretends suddenly to notice* **Romeo**'s *presence*] Ah! Signior Romeo! [*He sweeps his hat to the ground in an exaggerated gesture of fashionable politeness*] Bonjour! That's a French greeting for your French trousers. You cheated us last night.

**Romeo**    Good day to you both. How did I cheat you?

**Mercutio**    Gave us the slip, sir – the slip! Get it?

**Romeo**    Forgive me, good Mercutio. I had some pressing business, and in my special circumstances a man may skip politeness.

**Mercutio**    That's like saying that in a case like yours, a man can use his legs to bend the rules.

**Romeo**    [*bowing*] You mean curtsy?

**Mercutio**    That's it exactly!

**Romeo**    How courteously put!

**Mercutio**    Where courtesy's concerned, I'm the pink of perfection!

**Romeo**    'Pink' meaning flower?

**Mercutio**    Right!

**Romeo**    In that case, my shoe is very beautiful. [*He points to his shoes which have been 'pinked' with pinking-shears, to make them fashionably ornamental*]

**Mercutio**    Such wit! [*He has to cap it with a string of puns*] To follow your joke through: the bootiful shoe in which you are shod is so shoddy that when its sole sole is worn, nothing at last will remain but the joke, solely singular.

**Romeo**    Oh what a flimsy single-soled jest, singular solely for its silliness!

60 **Mercutio**    Come between us, good Benvolio; my wits faints.

**Romeo**    Swits and spurs, swits and spurs; or I'll cry a match.

**Mercutio**    Nay, if our wits run the wild-goose chase, I am
done; for thou hast more of the wild goose in one of thy wits
than, I am sure, I have in my whole five. Was I with you there
65    for the goose?

**Romeo**    Thou wast never with me for anything when thou
wast not there for the goose.

**Mercutio**    I will bite thee by the ear for that jest.

**Romeo**    Nay, good goose, bite not.

70 **Mercutio**    Thy wit is a very bitter sweeting; it is a most sharp
sauce.

**Romeo**    And is it not then well served in to a sweet goose?

**Mercutio**    O, here's a wit of cheveril, that stretches from an
inch narrow to an ell broad!

75 **Romeo**    I stretch it out for that word 'broad', which, added to
the goose, proves thee far and wide a broad goose.

**Mercutio**    Why, is not this better now than groaning for love?
Now art thou sociable, now art thou Romeo; now art thou
what thou art by art as well as by nature; for this drivelling
80    love is like a great natural that runs lolling up and down to
hide his bauble in a hole.

**Benvolio**    Stop there, stop there.

**Mercutio**    Thou desirest me to stop in my tale against the hair.

**Benvolio**    Thou wouldst else have made thy tale large.

85 **Mercutio**    O, thou art deceived: I would have made it short;
for I was come to the whole depth of my tale, and meant,
indeed, to occupy the argument no longer.

**Mercutio**   Part us, good Benvolio: my wits are flagging!

**Romeo**   [*not relenting: ready for more*] Whip and spurs! Keep going! Otherwise I've won!

**Mercutio**   Well, if our wits are running in a wild-goose chase, I've lost: you've got more of the goose in one of your wits than I have in my whole five! [*He sits, exhausted*] Have I cooked your goose? Are we even?

**Romeo**   You're never even with me, only odd, like a silly goose.

**Mercutio**   I'll bite your ear for that one!

**Romeo**   Good geese don't bite!

**Mercutio**   You've got a very saucy wit, like a bitter apple.

**Romeo**   Isn't sharp apple sauce what goes with a sweet goose?

**Mercutio**   A little bit of wit can be stretched a long way!

**Romeo**   I only stretch it out to prove you are known far and wide as a very big goose indeed!

**Mercutio**   Well now – isn't this better than groaning for love? Now you're being sociable! Now you are the real Romeo! Now 'Thou art what thou art' – by art as well as by nature. This drooling love is like a big soft lad who runs about with his tongue hanging out, looking for a hole to hide his toy in.

**Benvolio**   [*foreseeing a new round of witicisms*] Stop there! Stop there!

**Mercutio**   [*all innocent*] You want me to cut my tale short before I reach the best part?

**Benvolio**   Your tale would undoubtedly get bigger, otherwise.

**Mercutio**   You misunderstand: I'd have shortened it, because I had finished my tale and meant to argue no more.

**Romeo**    Here's goodly gear!

[*Enter* **Nurse** *and her man,* **Peter**]

**Mercutio**    A sail, a sail!

90 **Benvolio**    Two, two; a shirt and a smock.

**Nurse**    Peter!

**Peter**    Anon.

**Nurse**    My fan, Peter.

**Mercutio**    Good Peter, to hide her face; for her fan's the fairer
95    face.

**Nurse**    God ye good morrow, gentlemen.

**Mercutio**    God ye good den, fair gentlewoman.

**Nurse**    Is it good den?

**Mercutio**    'Tis no less, I tell ye; for the bawdy hand of the dial
100    is now upon the prick of noon.

**Nurse**    Out upon you! What a man are you?

**Romeo**    One, gentlewoman, that God hath made himself to
mar.

**Nurse**    By my troth, it is well said. 'For himself to mar' quoth
105    'a! Gentlemen, can any of you tell me where I may find the
young Romeo?

**Romeo**    I can tell you; but young Romeo will be older when
you have found him than he was when you sought him. I am
the youngest of that name, for fault of a worse.

110 **Nurse**    You say well.

[*The* **Nurse** *enters with her servant* **Peter**]

**Romeo**    [*mocking the* **Nurse***'s head-dress and voluminous garments*] Here's a splendid rig-out! [*Pretending she's a ship in full sail*] Sail ho!

**Mercutio**    Two, two! [*Referring to the Nurse's man*] His and hers!

**Nurse**    Peter!

**Peter**    Coming!

**Nurse**    My fan, Peter. [**Peter** *produces one from a bag he is carrying*]

**Mercutio**    It's to hide her face, Peter, the fan's the prettier!

**Nurse**    Good morning to you, gentlemen.

**Mercutio**    Good afternoon, dear madam.

**Nurse**    Is it afternoon already?

**Mercutio**    It is indeed. The bawdy hand of the clock is sticking right up at noon. [*He make's an indecent gesture with his forearm and fist to demonstrate*]

**Nurse**    Be off with you! What sort of a man are you?

**Romeo**    One, dear lady, whom God has made, for himself [*pointing to* **Mercutio**] to mar.

**Nurse**    Upon my word, that's well said! 'For himself to mar', you said! [*She looks at* **Mercutio** *disdainfully*] Gentlemen, can any of you tell me where I can find the young Romeo?

**Romeo**    I can tell you – but 'young Romeo' will be older when you've found him than he was when you looked for him. I'm the youngest of that name, for want of a . . . [*changing the well-known saying*] . . . worse.

**Nurse**    Well put.

113

**Mercutio**    Yea, is the worst well? Very well too, i' faith;
wisely, wisely.

**Nurse**    If you be he, sir, I desire some confidence with you.

**Benvolio**    She will indite him to some supper.

115 **Mercutio**    A bawd, a bawd, a bawd! So, ho!

**Romeo**    What hast thou found?

**Mercutio**    No hare, sir; unless a hare, sir, in a lenten pie, that
is something stale and hoar ere it be spent. [*He sings*]

> An old hare hoar,
120 > And an old hare hoar,
> Is very good meat in Lent;
> But a hare that is hoar
> Is too much for a score,
> When it hoars ere it be spent.

125 Romeo, will you come to your father's? We'll to dinner
thither.

**Romeo**    I will follow you.

**Mercutio**    Farewell ancient lady. Farewell, lady, lady, lady.

[*Exeunt* **Mercutio** *and* **Benvolio**]

**Nurse**    I pray you, sir, what saucy merchant was this that was
130 so full of his ropery?

**Romeo**    A gentleman, nurse, that loves to hear himself talk,
and will speak more in a minute than he will stand to in a
month.

**Mercutio**   Oh, so 'worse' is well put? Very shrewd. Most wise. Most wise.

**Nurse**   [*ignoring the sarcasm*] If you are him, sir, I'd like to speak to you conferentially.

**Benvolio**   [*mocking the **Nurse**'s misuse of words*] She wants to give him an 'intimation' to dinner!

**Mercutio**   [*tauntingly*] She's a whore! a whore! a whore! [*In a tone of discovery*] Aha!

**Romeo**   What, have you found a hare?

**Mercutio**   A whore! Not a hare! Unless it's a hare in a hoary old meat pie!   [*He sings*]

> A hairy old whore
> And an old hoar hare
> Are very good meat for Lent
> But a clapped-out whore
> Isn't useful any more
> To a pimp or a lusty gent.

Romeo, shall we go to your father's? We'll dine there.

**Romeo**   I'll follow you.

**Mercutio**   [*extravagantly polite*] Farewell ancient lady! [*He bows and scrapes as he leaves*] Lady . . . lady . . . lady . . . [*He turns a corner and leaves, with **Benvolio** following, laughing*]

**Nurse**   Tell me, sir, who was the smart alec with the smutty talk?

**Romeo**   A gentleman, Nurse, that loves the sound of his own voice. It would take a month to justify what he says in a minute.

**Nurse**   An 'a speak anything against me, I'll take him down,
135   and 'a were lustier than he is, and twenty such Jacks; and if I
cannot, I'll find those that shall. Scurvy knave! I am not of his
flirt-gills; I am none of his skains-mates. And thou must stand
by too, and suffer every knave to use me at his pleasure?

**Peter**   I saw no man use you at his pleasure. If I had, my
140   weapon should quickly have been out, I warrant you. I dare
draw as soon as another man, if I see occasion in a good
quarrel, and the law on my side.

**Nurse**   Now, afore God, I am so vexed that every part about
me quivers. Scurvy knave! Pray you sir, a word; and as I told
145   you, my young lady bid me enquire you out. What she bid me
say I will keep to myself. But first let me tell ye, if ye should
lead her in a fool's paradise, as they say, it were a very gross
kind of behaviour, as they say; for the gentlewoman is young,
and therefore, if you should deal double with her, truly it
150   were an ill thing to be offered to any gentlewoman, and very
weak dealing.

**Romeo**   Nurse, commend me to thy lady and mistress. I
protest unto thee –

**Nurse**   Good heart, and i' faith I will tell her as much. Lord,
155   Lord! She will be a joyful woman.

**Romeo**   What wilt thou tell her, nurse? Thou dost not mark
me.

**Nurse**   I will tell her, sir, that you do protest. Which, as I take
it, is a gentlemanlike offer.

160   **Romeo**   Bid her devise
Some means to come to shrift this afternoon,
And there she shall at Friar Lawrence' cell
Be shrived and married. Here is for thy pains.

**Nurse**   No, truly, sir; not a penny.

**Nurse**  If he says anything against me, I'll have him up, I will!
For all he's a hard knock! Or twenty such John Thomases! And
if I can't, I'll find those that can! The cheeky monkey! I'm not
one of his fancy-women! I'm no scrubber! [*To* **Peter**] And you
stand there, letting every Tom, Dick and Harry have his way
with me!

**Peter**  I didn't see any man have his way with you. If I had, I'd
have soon got my weapon out, I can tell you. I'm as quick as
the next man at getting it out if there's a chance of a good
quarrel, and the law's on my side.

**Nurse**  Now in God's name, I'm so vexed my parts are all of a
quiver! [*Hurling one last insult in the direction of the departed*
**Mercutio**] Cheeky monkey! [*To* **Romeo**] I'd like a word with
you, sir. As I told you, my young lady asked me to find your
whereabouts. What she told me to say, I'll keep to myself.
First, let me tell you that if you lead her up the garden path, as
the saying goes, that would be doing the dirty, as they say.
Madam is young, so if you double-cross her, that really would
be a nasty trick to play on any young lady; very shady dealing.

**Romeo**  Nurse, send my greetings to your lady and mistress. I
solemnly declare to you –

**Nurse**  Bless your heart! Indeed, I'll tell her so. Lord, lord, she'll
be a happy woman!

**Romeo**  What will you tell her, Nurse? You're not listening to
me –

**Nurse**  I'll tell her, sir, that you 'solemnly declare', and that's a
gentleman's proposal!

**Romeo**  Tell her to find some way to come to confession this
afternoon. There at Friar Lawrence's cell, she can both make
her confession and be married. [*He takes some money from
his purse*] This is for your trouble.

**Nurse**  No, honestly, sir – not a penny!

117

165 **Romeo**   Go to – I say you shall.

**Nurse**   This afternoon, sir? Well, she shall be there.

**Romeo**   And stay, good nurse – behind the abbey wall
Within this hour my man shall be with thee,
And bring thee cords made like a tackled stair,
170 Which to the high top-gallant of my joy
Must be my convoy in the secret night.
Farewell, be trusty, and I'll quit thy pains.
Farewell, commend me to thy mistress.

**Nurse**   Now God in heaven bless thee! Hark you sir.

175 **Romeo**   What say'st thou, my dear nurse?

**Nurse**   Is your man secret? Did you ne'er hear say
Two may keep counsel, putting one away?

**Romeo**   I warrant thee my man's as true as steel.

**Nurse**   Well, sir. My mistress is the sweetest lady – Lord,
180 Lord! when 'twas a little prating thing! O, there is a nobleman
in town, one Paris, that would fain lay knife aboard. But she,
good soul, had as lief see a toad, a very toad, as see him. I
anger her sometimes, and tell her that Paris is the properer
man. But, I'll warrant you, when I say so she looks as pale as
185 any clout in the versal world. Doth not rosemary and Romeo
begin both with a letter?

**Romeo**   Ay, nurse. What of that? Both with an R.

**Nurse**   Ah, mocker! That's the dog's name. R is for the – no, I
know it begins with some other letter. And she hath the
190 prettiest sententious of it, of you and rosemary, that it would
do you good to hear it.

**Romeo**   Commend me to thy lady.

**Nurse**   Ay, a thousand times. Peter!

**Romeo**    No really. I insist.

**Nurse**    [*taking it*] This afternoon, sir? She'll be there.

**Romeo**    Stay behind the abbey wall, good Nurse. Within the
hour, my man will join you, and bring you a rope ladder which
will enable me to reach the pinnacle of my joy in the dead of
night. Farewell. Keep our secret, and I'll reward you. Farewell.
My regards to your mistress.

**Nurse**    May God in heaven bless you! But listen, sir – [*she
beckons him to come nearer*]

**Romeo**    Yes, dear Nurse?

**Nurse**    Is your man trustworthy? Did you never hear it said
'Two can keep a secret if one doesn't know it'?

**Romeo**    I guarantee my man's as true as steel.

**Nurse**    Well, sir, my mistress is the sweetest lady – Lord, Lord,
when she was a little chatter-box! Oh, there's a nobleman in
this town – Paris by name – who'd love to be aboard the
lugger. But she, dear soul, would as soon see a toad, a very
toad, as see him. I anger her, sometimes, and tell her that Paris
is the better-looking man, but I swear to you, when I say so,
she looks whiter than the whitest sheet in the whole world.
Don't 'rosemary' and 'Romeo' start with the same letter?

**Romeo**    Yes, Nurse, but what of that? Both begin with an R.

**Nurse**    Ah, you're pulling my leg. 'R' is what dogs say. R is for –
no. I know it starts with some other letter. She's got a lovely
proverbial saying about you and rosemary – it'd do you good
to hear it!

**Romeo**    [*guiding her on her way*] My regards to your lady

**Nurse**    Yes, a thousand times! [*Summoning* **Peter** *to go before
her*] Peter!

**Peter**    Anon.

195  **Nurse**    Before and apace.

[*Exeunt*]

## Scene 5

*Capulet's orchard. Enter* **Juliet**

**Juliet**    The clock struck nine when I did send the nurse;
In half an hour she promised to return.
Perchance she cannot meet him. That's not so.
O she is lame! Love's heralds should be thoughts,
5    Which ten times faster glide than the sun's beams
Driving back shadows over louring hills;
Therefore do nimble-pinioned doves draw Love,
And therefore hath the wind-swift Cupid wings.
Now is the sun upon the highmost hill
10   Of this day's journey; and from nine till twelve
Is three long hours, yet she is not come.
Had she affections and warm youthful blood,
She would be as swift in motion as a ball.
My words would bandy her to my sweet love,
15   And his to me.
But old folks – many feign as they were dead,
Unwieldy, slow, heavy, and pale as lead.

[*Enter* **Nurse** *and* **Peter**]

O God, she comes! O honey nurse, what news?
Hast thou met with him? Send thy man away.

20  **Nurse**    Peter, stay at the gate.

[*Exit* **Peter**]

**Peter**    Coming!

**Nurse**    Lead the way, and with all speed!

[*They go their separate ways*]

## Scene 5

*The Capulet's garden.* **Juliet** *enters*

*Read* ——

**Juliet**    The clock was striking nine when I sent the Nurse. She promised to be back in half an hour. Perhaps she can't find him. That couldn't be! Oh, she's slow! Love's messengers should be like thoughts, which travel faster than retreating shadows when the sun's beams sweep a glowering hill. That's why swift-winged doves pull the chariot of Venus and why speedy Cupid has his wings. The sun is at high noon. From nine till twelve is three long hours, and still she isn't back. If she had emotions and youth's warm blood, she'd move as quickly as a ball. My words would hurl her to my sweet love, and his would throw her back again to me. But these old folk — many of them pretend to be dead. They're clumsy, slow, heavy, and pale as lead.

[**Peter** *comes in, followed by the* **Nurse**]

Oh God, she's here! Oh sweet Nurse! What news? Have you found him? Send your man away.

**Nurse**    [*bossily*] Peter, stay at the gate! [**Peter** *obediently departs*]

**Juliet**    Now, good sweet nurse – O Lord, why look'st thou sad?
Though news be sad, yet tell them merrrily.
If good, thou shamest the music of sweet news
25    By playing it to me with so sour a face.

**Nurse**    I am aweary! Give me leave a while.
Fie, how my bones ache! What a jaunce have I had!

**Juliet**    I would thou hadst my bones and I thy news.
Nay, come, I pray thee, speak. Good, good nurse, speak!

30 **Nurse**    Jesu, what haste! Can you not stay a while?
Do you not see that I am out of breath?

**Juliet**    How art thou out of breath, when thou hast breath
To say to me that thou art out of breath?
The excuse that thou dost make in this delay
35    Is longer than the tale thou dost excuse.
Is thy news good or bad? Answer to that.
Say either, and I'll stay the circumstance.
Let me be satisfied, is't good or bad?

**Nurse**    Well, you have made a simple choice! You know not
40    how to choose a man. Romeo! No, not he. Though his face be
better than any man's, yet his leg excels all men's. And for a
hand, and a foot, and a body, though they be not to be talked
on, yet they are past compare. He is not the flower of
courtesy, but I'll warrant him as gentle as a lamb. Go thy
45    ways, wench, serve God. What, have you dined at home?

**Juliet**    No, no. But all this did I know before.
What says he of our marriage? What of that?

**Nurse**    Lord, how my head aches! What a head have I!
It beats as it would fall in twenty pieces.
50    My back a t'other side! Ah, my back, my back!
Beshrew your heart for sending me about
To catch my death with jauncing up and down!

**Juliet**    Now, good sweet Nurse – [*she scans the* **Nurse***'s face for guidance*] Oh, Lord, why do you look so miserable? If the news is bad, tell it cheerfully. If it's good, you spoil the melody of welcome news by playing it with so sour a face!

**Nurse**    [*making the best of her star part*] I'm tired out. Give me a moment. [*She puffs and pants impressively*] My, how my bones ache! What a trip I've had!

**Juliet**    [*desperately impatient*] I wish you had my bones and I your news! Now come, I beg of you: tell me – good, good Nurse – tell me!

**Nurse**    Jesus! What haste! Can't you wait a moment? Don't you see I'm out of breath?

**Juliet**    How can you be out of breath when you've got breath to tell me you are out of breath? The excuse you're making to delay is longer than the tale itself. Is your news good or bad? Answer me that. Say one or the other, and I'll wait for the details. Settle my mind: is it good, or bad?

**Nurse**    Well, you've made a silly choice. You don't know how to choose a man. Romeo? No, not him. He's got a nicer face than any man's; a far better leg; and as for his hand, his foot and his body, though they're not worth talking about, they're beyond compare. He's not politeness itself, but I must say he's as gentle mannered as a lamb. Well, off you go, wench. Serve God. [*as if she's answered Juliet's question and the discussion is over*] Did you eat at home?

**Juliet**    No, no . . . But I knew all this before. What does he say about our marriage? What about that?

**Nurse**    [*still playing her game*] Lord, how my head aches! [*Holding her forehead*] Oh! my head! It's thumping as if it would break into twenty pieces. [*She winces*] My back on the other side. [*Her hand finds the spot*] Ah, my back, my back! Curse your heart for sending me all over the place, catching my death with jaunting up and down.

**Juliet**   I' faith, I am sorry that thou art not well.
Sweet, sweet, sweet nurse, tell me, what says my love?

55 **Nurse**   Your love says like an honest gentleman, and a
courteous, and a kind, and a handsome, and, I warrant, a
virtuous – Where is your mother?

**Juliet**   Where is my mother! Why, she is within.
Where should she be? How oddly thou repliest!
60 'Your love says like an honest gentleman,
"Where is your mother?" '

**Nurse**                          O God's lady dear!
Are you so hot? Marry, come up, I trow.
Is this the poultice for my aching bones?
Henceforward, do your messages yourself.

65 **Juliet**   Here's such a coil! Come, what says Romeo?

**Nurse**   Have you got leave to go to shrift to-day?

**Juliet**   I have.

**Nurse**   Then hie you hence to Friar Lawrence' cell.
There stays a husband to make you a wife.
70 Now comes the wanton blood up in your cheeks.
They'll be in scarlet straight at any news.
Hie you to church. I must another way
To fetch a ladder, by the which your love
Must climb a bird's nest soon when it is dark.
75 I am the drudge, and toil in your delight.
But you shall bear the burden soon at night.
Go. I'll to dinner. Hie you to the cell.

**Juliet**   Hie to high fortune! Honest nurse, farewell!

[*Exeunt*]

**Juliet**   Honestly, I'm sorry you aren't well. [*As persuasively as she can*] Sweet, sweet, sweet Nurse: do tell me. What did my love say?

**Nurse**   Your love says – like an honourable, courteous, kind, handsome and no doubt virtuous gentleman – [*The **Nurse** isn't ready to reveal all even yet*] Where's your mother?

**Juliet**   [*getting angry now*] Where is my mother? Why, she's inside the house. Where should she be? What an odd reply – 'Your love says, like an honourable gentleman, ''Where is your mother?'' '

**Nurse**   Oh by our dear Lady! Are you so impatient? Dear me! So this is the cure for my aching bones? In future, do your messages yourself!

**Juliet**   Such a fuss! Come now, what did Romeo say?

**Nurse**   Have you got permission to go to confession today?

**Juliet**   I have.

**Nurse**   [*businesslike at last*] Then go to Friar Lawrence's cell. There you'll find a husband to make you a wife. [**Juliet** *blushes at the news*] The blood rushes to your cheeks: any news will make them red. Off you go to church. I have to go another way, to fetch a ladder, by which your lover can go bird nesting after dark. I'm the drudge, labouring to make you happy. But you'll be doing all the work tonight. Go now. I'll have my dinner. Off with you to the cell!

**Juliet**   Off to good fortune! Farewell, honest Nurse!

## Scene 6

*Friar Lawrence's cell. Enter* **Friar Lawrence** *and* **Romeo**

**Friar Lawrence**    So smile the heavens upon this holy act
That after-hours with sorrow chide us not!

**Romeo**    Amen, amen! But come what sorrow can,
It cannot countervail the exchange of joy
5    That one short minute gives me in her sight.
Do thou but close our hands with holy words,
Then love-devouring death do what he dare.
It is enough I may but call her mine.

**Friar Lawrence**    These violent delights have violent ends,
10    And in their triumph die; like fire and powder,
Which, as they kiss, consume. The sweetest honey
Is loathsome in his own deliciousness,
And in the taste confounds the appetite.
Therefore love moderately: long love doth so;
15    Too swift arrives as tardy as too slow.

[*Enter* **Juliet**]

Here comes the lady. O, so light a foot
Will ne'er wear out the everlasting flint.
A lover may bestride the gossamer
That idles in the wanton summer air
20    And yet not fall, so light is vanity.

**Juliet**    Good even to my ghostly confessor.

**Friar Lawrence**    Romeo shall thank thee, daughter, for us
both.

**Juliet**    As much to him, else is his thanks too much.

# Scene 6

*Friar Lawrence's cell. Enter* **Friar Lawrence** *and* **Romeo**

**Friar Lawrence**   May heaven smile upon this holy ceremony, and may sorrow never punish us for it in days to come.

**Romeo**   Amen, amen. But whatever sorrow may come, it can never outweigh the joy from one short minute of seeing her. Just join our hands in holy matrimony, then love-consuming death can do whatever it dares. It's enough that I can call her mine.

**Friar Lawrence**   These violent passions have violent ends, and die at their peak; like fire and gunpowder which, meeting, destroy themselves. The sweetest honey is so delicious that it cloys the appetite, therefore, love in moderation if you want it to endure. In the long run, the hasty arrive no sooner than the slow.

[**Juliet** *enters*]

Here comes the lady. Her feet will never wear out life's hard road! A lover can walk across the gossamer strands of spiders' webs as they drift in the playful summer air, and still not fall: so insubstantial are the pleasures of this world.

**Juliet**   Good afternoon, Father.

**Friar Lawrence**   Romeo will thank you, daughter, on our behalf.

[**Romeo** *kisses her*]

**Juliet**   He needs some thanks back: [*She kisses him*] or else he has overpaid.

25 **Romeo**    Ah Juliet, if the measure of thy joy
       Be heaped like mine, and that thy skill be more
       To blazon it, then sweeten with thy breath
       This neighbour air, and let rich music's tongue
       Unfold the imagined happiness that both
30     Receive in either by this dear encounter.

   **Juliet**    Conceit, more rich in matter than in words,
       Brags of his substance, not of ornament.
       They are but beggars that can count their worth;
       But my true love is grown to such excess
35     I cannot sum up sum of half my wealth.

   **Friar Lawrence**    Come, come with me, and we will make short
       work.
       For, by your leaves, you shall not stay alone
       Till holy church incorporate two in one.

                                                        [*Exeunt*]

**Romeo**   Ah, Juliet! If your joy is as great as mine, and your powers of communication greater, speak with your sweet breath the precious words that describe the mutual happiness of our dear meeting!

**Juliet**   The richness of reality speaks more eloquently than fine words. Only love's beggars can count their wealth. My true love has grown so vastly rich I couldn't calculate the half of it.

**Friar Lawrence**   Come. Come with me, and we'll get down to business. For, begging your pardons, you can't be left alone until you have been united in marriage by the Holy Church.

[*They leave*]

# Act three

## Scene 1

*Enter* **Mercutio, Benvolio** *and* **Men**

**Benvolio**    I pray thee, good Mercutio, let's retire;
The day is hot, the Capels are abroad,
And if we meet we shall not 'scape a brawl,
For now these hot days is the mad blood stirring.

5  **Mercutio**    Thou art like one of these fellows that, when he
enters the confines of a tavern, claps me his sword upon the
table and says 'God send me no need of thee!' and by the
operation of the second cup draws him on the drawer, when
indeed there is no need.

10  **Benvolio**    Am I like such a fellow?

**Mercutio**    Come, come, thou art as hot a Jack in thy mood as
any in Italy; and as soon moved to be moody, and as soon
moody to be moved.

**Benvolio**    And what to?

15  **Mercutio**    Nay, and there were two such, we should have none
shortly, for one would kill the other. Thou? Why, thou wilt
quarrel with a man that hath a hair more or a hair less in his
beard than thou hast. Thou wilt quarrel with a man for
cracking nuts, having no other reason but because thou hast
20  hazel eyes. What eye but such an eye would spy out such a
quarrel? Thy head is as full of quarrels as an egg is full of
meat, and yet thy head hath been beaten as addle as an egg for
quarrelling. Thou hast quarrelled with a man for coughing in
the street, because he hath wakened thy dog that hath lain
25  asleep in the sun. Didst thou not fall out with a tailor for

# Act three

## Scene 1

*A street. Enter* **Mercutio**, *his* **Page, Benvolio** *and servants*

**Benvolio**  Good Mercutio, let's go home. It's hot, and the Capulets are on the streets. If we meet, we can't avoid a brawl. These hot days make the mad blood stir.

**Mercutio**  You're like one of those fellows who slaps down his sword on the table when he enters a tavern, and says 'I hope to God I don't need you.' By the time he's had two drinks, he's drawn his sword against the barman, when there is no need!

**Benvolio**  Am I like that?

**Mercutio**  Come, come: when the mood takes you, you're as hotblooded a character as anyone in Italy: soon provoked to anger, and touchy enough to be provoked.

**Benvolio**  To what?

**Mercutio**  [*deliberately misunderstanding the 'To'*] Now if there were two of you, we'd soon have none, for one would kill the other! You? Why, you'd quarrel over whether a man has one hair more or one hair less in his beard than you have! You'd quarrel with a man for cracking nuts, just because you've got hazel eyes! Whose eye but yours would see a quarrel in that? Your head is as full of quarrels as an egg is full of food – yet you've had your head bashed like an addled egg for your quarrelling. You've quarrelled with a man for coughing in the street because he's wakened up your dog lying asleep in the sun! Didn't you quarrel with a tailor

wearing his new doublet before Easter; with another for tying
his new shoes with old riband? And yet thou wilt tutor me
from quarrelling!

**Benvolio**    And I were so apt to quarrel as thou art, any man
30    should buy the fee simple of my life for an hour and a quarter.

**Mercutio**    The fee simple! O simple!

[*Enter* **Tybalt** *and others*]

**Benvolio**    By my head, here come the Capulets.

**Mercutio**    By my heel, I care not.

**Tybalt**    Follow me close, for I will speak to them.
35    Gentlemen, good e'en: a word with one of you.

**Mercutio**    And but one word with one of us? Couple it with
something, make it a word and a blow.

**Tybalt**    You shall find me apt enough to that, sir, and you will
give me occasion.

40 **Mercutio**    Could you not take some occasion without giving?

**Tybalt**    Mercutio, thou consortest with Romeo.

**Mercutio**    Consort? What, dost thou make us minstrels? And
thou make minstrels of us, look to hear nothing but discords.
Here's my fiddlestick, here's that shall make you dance.
45    Zounds, consort!

**Benvolio**    We talk here in the public haunt of men.
Either withdraw unto some private place,
Or reason coldly of your grievances,
Or else depart. Here all eyes gaze on us.

because he wore new clothes before Easter? And with someone else for tying new shoes with old laces? And yet you'll lecture me about quarrelling!

**Benvolio**    If I were as inclined to quarrel as you are, my life wouldn't be worth an hour and a quarter's outright purchase, or 'fee-simple'.

**Mercutio**    [*mocking the legal term*] Fee-simple? Very simple!

[**Tybalt** *enters with his followers*]

**Benvolio**    [*alarmed*] By heaven, here come the Capulets!

**Mercutio**    By hell, I couldn't care less.

**Tybalt**    [*to his followers*] Keep close behind. I'm going to speak to them. [*To* **Mercutio** *and* **Benviolo**] Gentlemen. Good evening. A word with one of you.

**Mercutio**    Just one word between two of us? Join it up with something. Make it a word and a blow?

**Tybalt**    Just give me an excuse, sir, and you won't find me wanting.

**Mercutio**    Couldn't you make an excuse, without my giving you one?

**Tybalt**    Mercutio, you're one of Romeo's group –

**Mercutio**    Group? [*He mocks the word*] Oh, so we're a group of musicians, are we? Make musicians of us, and don't be surprised if you get discord! [*Tapping his sword*] Here's my instrument. That'll have you dancing! [*He snorts contemptuously*] 'Group'!

**Benvolio**    [*embarrassed*] We're talking here in the open street. Either let's go somewhere private, or argue calmly about your difference, or break it up. Here, everyone's looking at us.

50 **Mercutio**    Men's eyes were made to look, and let them gaze.
I will not budge for no man's pleasure, I.

[*Enter* **Romeo**]

**Tybalt**    Well, peace be with you, sir, here comes my man.

**Mercutio**    But I'll be hanged, sir, if he wear your livery.
Marry, go before to field, he'll be your follower.
55 Your worship in that sense may call him 'man'.

**Tybalt**    Romeo, the love I bear thee can afford
No better term than this: thou art a villain.

**Romeo**    Tybalt, the reason that I have to love thee
Doth much excuse the appertaining rage
60 To such a greeting: villain am I none,
Therefore farewell. I see thou knowest me not.

**Tybalt**    Boy, this shall not excuse the injuries
That thou hast done me, therefore turn and draw.

**Romeo**    I do protest I never injured thee,
65 But love thee better than thou canst devise
Till thou shalt know the reason of my love.
And so, good Capulet, which name I tender
As dearly as mine own, be satisfied.

**Mercutio**    O calm, dishonourable, vile submission:
70 Alla stoccata carries it away! [*He draws*]
Tybalt, you rat-catcher, will you walk?

**Tybalt**    What wouldst thou have with me?

**Mercutio**    Good King of Cats, nothing but one of your nine
lives that I mean to make bold withal, and as you shall use me
75 hereafter, dry-beat the rest of the eight. Will you pluck your
sword out of his pilcher by the ears? Make haste, lest mine be
about your ears ere it be out.

**Mercutio**   Men's eyes were made for looking, so let them stare. I won't budge to please any man. Not me.

[**Romeo** *enters*]

**Tybalt**   [*to* **Mercutio**, *icily*] Well, peace be with you, sir. Here comes the very man I was after.

**Mercutio**   [*twisting his words*] You won't recruit him, believe me! Set off for the battlefield, and yes, he'll follow you. In that sense he's 'your man' – [*sarcastically*] Your Worship!

**Tybalt**   Romeo: such is my regard for you that I can say no more than this: you are a villain!

**Romeo**   Tybalt, I've reason to be friends with you, and that restrains my anger at such a greeting. I'm not a villain. Therefore, goodbye. I realize you don't know me. [*He turns to go*]

**Tybalt**   That's no excuse for the insults you've given me, sonny! [*He draws his sword*] So turn and draw!

**Romeo**   [*not responding*] I swear I haven't offended you. I'm fonder of you than you can possibly imagine, till you know the reason why. So, good Capulet – a name I value as dearly as my own – be satisfied with that.

**Mercutio**   [*thinking this is cowardice*] Oh, what a calm, dishonourable and vile reply! The fancy fencer wins! [*He draws his sword, and mocks the coincidence that 'Tybalt' is a pet cat's name*] Tybalt, you rat-catcher: will you step aside?

**Tybalt**   What's your business with me?

**Mercutio**   [*rubbing the insult in*] Good King of Cats, I just want one of your nine lives! And I'll give the other eight a rough time, if you don't treat me better in future! Would you care to lug your sword from its sheath? Quick – or I'll cut your ears off before it's out!

**Tybalt**   I am for you. [*He draws*]

**Romeo**   Gentle Mercutio, put thy rapier up.

80 **Mercutio**   Come sir, your passado. [*They fight*]

**Romeo**   Draw, Benvolio, beat down their weapons.
Gentlemen, for shame, forbear this outrage.
Tybalt! Mercutio! The Prince expressly hath
Forbid this bandying in Verona streets.
85   Hold, Tybalt! Good Mercutio!

[**Tybalt** *under* **Romeo**'s *arm thrusts* **Mercutio** *in*]

[*Exit* **Tybalt** *with his followers*]

**Mercutio**   I am hurt.
A plague o' both your houses. I am sped.
Is he gone, and hath nothing?

**Benvolio**                                What, art thou hurt?

90 **Mercutio**   Ay, ay, a scratch, a scratch. Marry, 'tis enough.
Where's my page? Go villain, fetch a surgeon.

[*Exit* **Page**]

**Romeo**   Courage man, the hurt cannot be much.

**Mercutio**   No, 'tis not so deep as a well, nor so wide as a church
door, but 'tis enough, 'twill serve. Ask for me tomorrow and
95   you shall find me a grave man. I am peppered, I warrant, for
this world. A plague o' both your houses. Zounds, a dog, a
rat, a mouse, a cat, to scratch a man to death. A braggart, a
rogue, a villain, that fights by the book of arithmetic – why the
devil came you between us? I was hurt under your arm.

**Tybalt**  [*drawing*] I'm for you!

**Romeo**  [*alarmed*] Gentle Mercutio, put your sword back!

**Mercutio**  [*ignoring him: to* **Tybalt**] Come, sir, let's see your
classy strokes!

[**Mercutio** *and* **Tybalt** *fight*]

**Romeo**  Draw your sword, Benvolio, make them drop their
weapons! [*Trying to intercede*] Gentlemen, shame on you!
Stop this fighting! Tybalt! Mercutio! The Prince has
specifically banned this brawling in Verona's streets! Stop,
Tybalt! Good Mercutio – [*He steps between them.* **Tybalt**,
*shielded by* **Romeo**, *wounds* **Mercutio**]

[**Tybalt** *runs away, followed by his men*]

**Mercutio**  [*holding his wound*] I'm hurt. Damn your houses,
both! I'm done for. Has he gone? Scot-free?

**Benvolio**  Are you hurt?

**Mercutio**  Yes, oh, yes. A scratch. A scratch. But it's enough.
Where's my page? [*Mercutio's* **Page** *rushes forward*] Go, you
rogue, and get me a doctor.

[*The* **Page** *runs off*]

**Romeo**  Chin up, man. It can't be very bad.

**Mercutio**  [*with his usual dry wit, in spite of his pain*] No, it's not
as deep as a well, or as wide as a church door, but it's enough.
It'll do. Ask around for me tomorrow, and you'll find I'm a
'grave' man. I'm finished as far as this world's concerned, I
think. Damn both your houses! Christ! For a dog, a rat, a
mouse, a *cat* to scratch a man to death! A braggart, a rogue, a
villain who fights by the text-book! [*suddenly fierce, to*
**Romeo**] Why the hell did you come between us? He got me
under your arm.

137

100   **Romeo**    I thought all for the best.

**Mercutio**    Help me into some house, Benvolio,
Or I shall faint. A plague o' both your houses,
They have made worms' meat of me.
I have it, and soundly too. Your houses!

[*Exit* **Mercutio** *with* **Benvolio**]

105   **Romeo**    This gentleman, the Prince's near ally,
My very friend, hath got this mortal hurt
In my behalf – my reputation stained
With Tybalt's slander – Tybalt that an hour
Hath been my cousin. O sweet Juliet,
110   Thy beauty hath made me effeminate
And in my temper softened valour's steel.

[*Enter* **Benvolio**]

**Benvolio**    O Romeo, Romeo, brave Mercutio is dead.
That gallant spirit hath aspired the clouds
Which too untimely here did scorn the earth.

115   **Romeo**    This day's black fate on more days doth depend:
This but begins the woe others must end.

[*Enter* **Tybalt**]

**Benvolio**    Here comes the furious Tybalt back again.

**Romeo**    Alive, in triumph, and Mercutio slain.
Away to heaven respective lenity,
120   And fire-eyed fury be my conduct now!
Now Tybalt, take the 'villain' back again
That late thou gav'st me, for Mercutio's soul
Is but a little way above our heads,

**Romeo**    I thought it was all for the best.

**Mercutio**    Help me into a house, Benvolio, or I'll faint. Damn both your houses! They've made worms-meat of me! I've had it, well and truly. [*He winces*] Your houses!

[**Benvolio** *helps him out*]

**Romeo**    This fine man, the Prince's near relative, my true friend, got this mortal wound on my behalf – Tybalt having slandered me – Tybalt, my relative since an hour ago! Oh, Juliet: your beauty has unmanned me; softened the steel within my character!

[**Benvolio** *returns*]

**Benvolio**    Oh, Romeo, Romeo! Brave Mercutio is dead! The gallant soul has left the earth he scorned, and far too young has gone to heaven!

**Romeo**    After this black day, darker ones will follow. This is only the beginning of the sorrow that later days will end.

[**Tybalt** *returns, sword drawn*]

**Benvolio**    Here comes that fiery Tybalt back again!

**Romeo**    Alive, triumphant, and Mercutio dead! Let gentleness take itself off to heaven. Hot anger guides me from now on. Right, Tybalt! Take your 'villain' insult back again! Mercutio's soul is hovering just above our heads, waiting for your own to

Staying for thine to keep him company.
125 Either thou, or I, or both must go with him.

**Tybalt**    Thou wretched boy, that didst consort him here,
Shalt with him hence.

**Romeo**                              This shall determine that.

[*They fight*. **Tybalt** *falls*]

**Benvolio**    Romeo, away, be gone,
The citizens are up, and Tybalt slain!
130 Stand not amazed. The Prince will doom thee death
If thou art taken. Hence, be gone, away!

**Romeo**    O, I am fortune's fool.

**Benvolio**                          Why dost thou stay?

[*Exit* **Romeo**]

[*Enter* **Citizens**]

**Citizen**    Which way ran he that killed Mercutio?
Tybalt, that murderer, which way ran he?

**Benvolio**    There lies that Tybalt.

135 **Citizen**                          Up, sir, go with me.
I charge thee in the Prince's name obey.

[*Enter* **Prince, Montague, Capulet,** *their* **Wives** *and all*]

**Prince**    Where are the vile beginners of this fray?

**Benvolio**    O noble Prince, I can discover all
The unlucky manage of this fatal brawl.
140 There lies the man, slain by young Romeo,
That slew thy kinsman brave Mercutio.

keep it company. One or both of us must go with him!

**Tybalt**    You lousy brat: you were one of his gang, stick with him now!

**Romeo**    [*pulling out his sword*] This will decide that!

[*They fight furiously.* **Romeo**'s *sword strikes home, and* **Tybalt** *falls dead.* **Romeo** *stands transfixed*]

**Benvolio**    [*appalled*] Romeo – Get lost! Run! People are coming! Tybalt's dead! Don't stand there staring. The Prince will have your life if you're caught! Get going! Run!

**Romeo**    Oh, I'm luck's stupid fool! [*He still can't move*]

**Benvolio**    [*pushing him along*] What's keeping you?

[**Romeo** *comes to himself and runs*]

[*People arrive in hot pursuit of* **Tybalt**]

**Citizen**    Which way did Mercutio's killer go? Tybalt, that murderer, which way did he go?

**Benvolio**    There lies Tybalt.

**Citizen**    [*Not realizing what has happened*] Get up, sir. Come along with me. [*The* **Prince** *enters, followed by* **Montague**, **Capulet**, *their* **Wives**, *and followers*]

**Prince**    Where are the rogues who started all this?

**Benvolio**    Oh, noble Prince: I can tell you all the unfortunate details of this fatal brawl. [*Pointing to* **Tybalt**] There lies the man – killed by young Romeo – who killed your relative, the brave Mercutio.

**Lady Capulet**    Tybalt, my cousin, O my brother's child!
O Prince, O husband, O, the blood is spilled
Of my dear kinsman. Prince, as thou art true,
145 For blood of ours shed blood of Montague.
O cousin, cousin!

**Prince**    Benvolio, who began this bloody fray?

**Benvolio**    Tybalt, here slain, whom Romeo's hand did slay.
Romeo, that spoke him fair, bid him bethink
150 How nice the quarrel was, and urged withal
Your high displeasure. All this uttered
With gentle breath, calm look, knees humbly bowed,
Could not take truce with the unruly spleen
Of Tybalt, deaf to peace, but that he tilts
155 With piercing steel at bold Mercutio's breast,
Who, all as hot, turns deadly point to point
And, with a martial scorn, with one hand beats
Cold death aside, and with the other sends
It back to Tybalt, whose dexterity
160 Retorts it. Romeo, he cries aloud
'Hold, friends! Friends part!' and swifter than his tongue
His agile arm beats down their fatal points
And twixt them rushes; underneath whose arm
An envious thrust from Tybalt hit the life
165 Of stout Mercutio; and then Tybalt fled,
But by and by comes back to Romeo,
Who had but newly entertained revenge,
And to't they go like lightning: for, ere I
Could draw to part them, was stout Tybalt slain,
170 And as he fell did Romeo turn and fly.
This is the truth, or let Benvolio die.

**Lady Capulet**   [*on her knees beside the body of* **Tybalt**] My nephew Tybalt! My brother's son! Oh, Prince! Oh, husband! [*She sobs in grief*] Oh, the blood of my dear kinsman has been spilled! [*On her knees, begging*] Oh Prince, as you are just: for the death we've suffered, a Montague must die! [*Weeping over the body*] Oh, nephew, nephew!

**Prince**   Benvolio, who started this blood-shed?

**Benvolio**   Tybalt, here lying dead, who was killed by Romeo. Romeo, who spoke politely to him, told him to consider how trivial the quarrel was, and stressed how angry you yourself would be. In spite of saying all this gently, calmly, and on bended knee, he couldn't pacify the wild hostility of Tybalt, who just wouldn't listen. On the contrary, he thrust his rapier at bold Mercutio's chest, who just as angry, drew his weapon in response. With soldierly skill, his left hand defended by a dagger, Mercutio lunged with his rapier in his right; Tybalt deftly countered this. Romeo shouted 'Stop, friends! Break!' and before he'd finished speaking he'd knocked their swords down and rushed beween them. Under cover of Romeo's arm, a malicious thrust from Tybalt took brave Mercutio's life, and Tybalt ran away. But very soon he returned to Romeo, who only at that point thought of revenge. They set upon each other with the speed of lightning, and before I could draw my sword to part them, brave Tybalt was slain. As he fell, Romeo turned and fled. This is the truth, on my life.

**Lady Capulet**    He is a kinsman to the Montague.
Affection makes him false. He speaks not true.
Some twenty of them fought in this black strife
175 And all those twenty could but kill one life.
I beg for justice, which thou, Prince, must give.
Romeo slew Tybalt. Romeo must not live.

**Prince**    Romeo slew him, he slew Mercutio.
Who now the price of his dear blood doth owe?

180 **Montague**    Not Romeo, Prince, he was Mercutio's friend.
His fault concludes but what the law should end,
The life of Tybalt.

**Prince**                    And for that offence
Immediately we do exile him hence.
I have an interest in your hearts' proceeding;
185 My blood for your rude brawls doth lie a-bleeding.
But I'll amerce you with so strong a fine
That you shall all repent the loss of mine.
I will be deaf to pleading and excuses.
Nor tears nor prayers shall purchase out abuses.
190 Therefore, use none. Let Romeo hence in haste,
Else, when he is found, that hour is his last.
Bear hence this body, and attend our will.
Mercy but murders, pardoning those that kill.

[*Exeunt*]

**Lady Capulet**    He's related to Romeo. Friendship makes him a
liar. He's not speaking the truth. About twenty of them fought
in this vile brawl, and all those twenty could only take one life. I
plead for justice, which you the Prince must give. Romeo killed
Tybalt. Romeo must die.

**Prince**    Romeo did kill Tybalt. But Tybalt killed Mercutio. Who
pays the price for his death?

**Montague**    Not Romeo, Prince. He was Mercutio's friend. He
only did what the law would have done: took the life of Tybalt.

**Prince**    And for that offence, we banish him immediately. I have
a personal interest in your vendetta: a relative of mine lies
bleeding because of your rowdy brawls. I'll fine you so heavily
that you'll all regret my loss. [*The* **Montagues** *and* **Capulets**
*protest*] I won't listen to your pleadings and excuses. Neither
tears nor prayers can buy off the judgement of the law, so
don't try them. Let Romeo go with all speed: if we find him,
that hour will be his last. Take this body away: await our
pleasure. To pardon murder is to encourage it.

[*They all leave*]

## Scene 2

*Juliet's room*


[*Enter* **Juliet**]

**Juliet**    Gallop apace, you fiery-footed steeds,
Towards Phoebus' lodging. Such a waggoner
As Phaeton would whip you to the west
And bring in cloudy night immediately.
5      Spread thy close curtain, love-performing night,
That runaway's eyes may wink, and Romeo
Leap to these arms untalked-of and unseen.
Lovers can see to do their amorous rite
By their own beauties; or, if love be blind,
10     It best agrees with night. Come, civil night,
Thou sober-suited matron, all in black,
And learn me how to lose a winning match
Played for a pair of stainless maidenhoods.
Hood my unmanned blood, bating in my cheeks,
15     With thy black mantle, till strange love grow bold,
Think true love acted simple modesty.
Come night, come Romeo, come thou day in night.
For thou wilt lie upon the wings of night
Whiter than new snow upon a raven's back.
20     Come gentle night, come loving black-browed night,
Give me my Romeo; and when he shall die
Take him and cut him out in little stars,
And he will make the face of heaven so fine
That all the world will be in love with night,
25     And pay no worship to the garish sun.
O, I have bought the mansion of a love
But not possessed it, and though I am sold,
Not yet enjoyed. So tedious is this day

## Scene 2

*Juliet's bedroom.* **Juliet** *is waiting at the window*


**Juliet**   If only sunset would come sooner! Young Phaeton, the
sun-god's son, now he could hasten it, and make it start
immediately! May night that's used for love fall soon, so that
eloping lovers may sleep, and Romeo can leap into my arms
silently and without my seeing him. Lovers can make love by
the light of their own radiance: or, if love is blind, it finds night
quite congenial. Come, virtuous night, you respectable old
lady dressed in solemn black – show me how I can both win
and lose this contest, played with our virginities as stakes.
Hide my blushing cheeks beneath your black cloak, till I
overcome my inexperience and turn the practice of true love
into an act of simple modesty. Come, night, come, Romeo!
Come, light of my night! You'll make the darkness seem
whiter than freshly fallen snow on the back of a raven. Come,
gentle night! Come, loving though black browed night! Give
me my Romeo; and when he dies, take him and cut him out
into little stars: he'll make the sky look so beautiful that all the
world will be in love with night, and cease its worship of the
glaring sun. Oh, I've bought a house called 'Love', but not yet
occupied it! Though I've been sold, I haven't given the owner
any pleasure! This day is never-ending, like the night before a

As is the night before some festival
30  To an impatient child that hath new robes
And may not wear them. O, here comes my Nurse.

[*Enter* **Nurse** *with cords, wringing her hands*]

And she brings news, and every tongue that speaks
But Romeo's name speaks heavenly eloquence.
Now, Nurse, what news? What hast thou there?
The cords that Romeo bid thee fetch?

35 **Nurse**                                          Ay, ay, the cords.

**Juliet**   Ay me, what news? Why dost thou wring thy hands?

**Nurse**   Ah well-a-day, he's dead, he's dead, he's dead!
We are undone, lady, we are undone.
Alack the day, he's gone, he's killed, he's dead.

**Juliet**   Can heaven be so envious?

40 **Nurse**                                          Romeo can,
Though heaven cannot. O Romeo, Romeo,
Who ever would have thought it? Romeo!

**Juliet**   What devil art thou that dost torment me thus?
This torture should be roared in dismal hell.
45  Hath Romeo slain himself? Say thou but 'Ay'
And that bare vowel 'I' shall poison more
Than the death-darting eye of cockatrice.
I am not I if there be such an 'Ay'.
Or those eyes shut that makes thee answer 'Ay'.
50  If he be slain say 'Ay', or if not, 'No'.
Brief sounds determine of my weal or woe.

**Nurse**   I saw the wound, I saw it with mine eyes –
God save the mark – here on his manly breast.
A piteous corse, a bloody piteous corse,
55  Pale, pale as ashes, all bedaubed in blood –
All in gore-blood. I swounded at the sight.

party to an impatient child that has new clothes, but can't yet wear them! Oh, here comes my Nurse.

[*Enter the* **Nurse** *with a rope ladder*]

And she brings news. Every mention of Romeo's name is divinely eloquent. Now, Nurse, what's the news? What have you got there? The ropes that Romeo asked you to bring?

**Nurse**    [*distressed*] Yes, yes. The ropes.

**Juliet**    Oh dear, what's happened? Why are you wringing your hands?

**Nurse**    [*weeping*] Alas, he's dead! He's dead, he's dead, he's dead! We're ruined, my lady, we're ruined! Alas, he's gone! He's killed! He's dead!

**Juliet**    Could heaven be so jealous?

**Nurse**    Romeo could, though heaven couldn't. Oh, Romeo! Romeo! Whoever would have believed it? Romeo!

**Juliet**    What kind of a devil are you to torment me like this? This is torture fit for murky hell. Has Romeo killed himself? Just say 'Ay', and that simple vowel 'I' will be more lethal to me than the legendary cockatrice's eye. I shall cease to be 'I' if 'Ay' is correct, or his eyes are closed who made you answer 'Ay'. If he's been killed, say 'Ay'. If not, 'No'. Happiness or misery depends on a simple word.

**Nurse**    I saw the wound. I saw it with my own eyes – God forgive me! – here on his manly breast. [*She demonstrates*] A pitiful corpse, a bloody pitiful corpse, pale, pale as ashes, all daubed with blood, all clotted blood. I fainted at the sight!

**Juliet**    O break, my heart. Poor bankrupt, break at once.
To prison, eyes, ne'er look on liberty.
Vile earth to earth resign, end motion here,
60    And thou and Romeo press one heavy bier.

**Nurse**    O Tybalt, Tybalt, the best friend I had.
O courteous Tybalt, honest gentleman!
That ever I should live to see thee dead!

**Juliet**    What storm is this that blows so contrary?
65    Is Romeo slaughtered and is Tybalt dead?
My dearest cousin and my dearer lord?
Then dreadful trumpet sound the general doom,
For who is living if those two are gone?

**Nurse**    Tybalt is gone, and Romeo banished.
70    Romeo that killed him, he is banished.

**Juliet**    O God! Did Romeo's hand shed Tybalt's blood?

**Nurse**    It did, it did, alas the day, it did.

**Juliet**    O serpent heart, hid with a flowering face.
Did ever dragon keep so fair a cave?
75    Beautiful tyrant, fiend angelical,
Dove-feathered raven, wolfish-ravening lamb!
Despised substance of divinest show!
Just opposite to what thou justly seem'st!
A damned saint, an honourable villain!
80    O nature what hadst thou to do in hell
When thou didst bower the spirit of a fiend
In mortal paradise of such sweet flesh?
Was ever book containing such vile matter
So fairly bound? O, that deceit should dwell
In such a gorgeous palace.

85 **Nurse**                    There's no trust,
No faith, no honesty in men. All perjured,
All forsworn, all naught, all dissemblers.

**Juliet**    My heart must break. Poor bankrupt heart, break right now. My eyes will never look upon liberty again, so off to prison they must go. My earthly body must return to earth, life must end, to share with Romeo one heavy funeral bed!

**Nurse**    [*preoccupied with her own thoughts*] Oh, Tybalt! Tybalt! The best friend I had! Oh, courteous Tybalt! Upright gentleman! That I should ever live to see you dead!

**Juliet**    Is there no end to our misfortune? Is Romeo murdered and is Tybalt dead? My dear cousin, and my even dearer husband? Let the trumpet sound the end of the world: who is living if these two are dead?

**Nurse**    Tybalt is dead, and Romeo banished. Romeo, who killed him, is banished!

**Juliet**    Oh God! Did Romeo kill Tybalt?

**Nurse**    He did, he did. Alas the day, he did!

**Juliet**    His handsome looks disguised a serpent's heart. What monster ever concealed itself so well? Charming ruffian! Angelic devil! Dove-like raven! Killer lamb! Evil pretending to be divinely good! The exact opposite of what you seem to be: a saint that's damned, a villain affecting to be honourable! Oh Nature! What were you doing in hell to embody the spirit of a fiend inside such a paradise of human loveliness? Was there ever such a distasteful book in such an attractive cover? Oh that deceit should enjoy such splendid surroundings!

**Nurse**    There's no trust or loyalty or honesty in men! They're all liars, all deceivers, all wicked, all cheats! Where's Peter? I need

Ah, where's my man? Give me some aqua vitae.
These griefs, these woes, these sorrows make me old.
Shame come to Romeo.

90 **Juliet**                              Blistered be thy tongue
For such a wish. He was not born to shame.
Upon his brow shame is ashamed to sit,
For 'tis a throne where honour may be crowned
Sole monarch of the universal earth.
95 O, what a beast was I to chide at him.

**Nurse**    Will you speak well of him that killed your cousin?

**Juliet**    Shall I speak ill of him that is my husband?
Ah, poor my lord, what tongue shall smooth thy name
When I thy three-hours wife have mangled it?
100 But wherefore, villain, didst thou kill my cousin?
That villain cousin would have killed my husband.
Back, foolish tears, back to your native spring,
Your tributary drops belong to woe
Which you mistaking offer up to joy.
105 My husband lives, that Tybalt would have slain,
And Tybalt's dead, that would have slain my husband.
All this is comfort. Wherefore weep I then?
Some word there was, worser than Tybalt's death,
That murdered me. I would forget it fain,
110 But O, it presses to my memory
Like damned guilty deeds to sinners' minds.
Tybalt is dead and Romeo – banished.
That 'banished', that one word 'banished',
Hath slain ten thousand Tybalts: Tybalt's death
115 Was woe enough, if it had ended there.
Or if sour woe delights in fellowship
And needly will be ranked with other griefs,
Why followed not, when she said 'Tybalt's dead',
Thy father or thy mother, nay or both,
120 Which modern lamentation might have moved?

some brandy! These griefs, these miseries, these sorrows, make me old. Shame on Romeo!

**Juliet**   [*fiercely loyal in spite of her own previous criticisms*] May your tongue be blistered for saying that! Shame isn't in his nature! Shame would be ashamed to show its face. In him, honour reigns supreme. Oh what a beast I was to scold him!

**Nurse**   Will you speak well of the man who killed your cousin?

**Juliet**   Shall I speak ill of the man who is my husband? My poor husband! Who'll clear your name, when I, your wife these last three hours, have sullied it? But why, villain, did you kill my cousin? Because that villainous cousin would have killed my husband! These foolish tears must stop: their source is sorrow, but I'm shedding them for joy. My husband is alive; Tybalt would have killed him. Tybalt is dead: he would have killed my husband. This is comforting. Why, therefore, am I crying? There was one word uttered, worse than Tybalt's death, which murdered me. I would gladly forget it, but alas it sticks in my memory like foul deeds in the minds of sinners. 'Tybalt is dead, and Romeo – banished.' That 'banished', that one word 'banished', is as bad as ten thousand slaughtered Tybalts. Tybalt's death was sorrowful enough if it had ended there. But, if bitter grief needs company, and has to be ranked with other sorrows, why, when she said 'Tybalt's dead', didn't she add 'and your father', or 'your mother', or even both? That would have provoked the normal floods of tears. But to follow

But with a rearward following Tybalt's death,
'Romeo is banished': to speak that word
Is father, mother, Tybalt, Romeo, Juliet,
All slain, all dead. Romeo is banished.
125  There is no end, no limit, measure, bound,
In that word's death. No words can that woe sound.
Where is my father and my mother, Nurse?

**Nurse**   Weeping and wailing over Tybalt's corse.
Will you go to them? I will bring you thither.

130 **Juliet**   Wash they his wounds with tears? Mine shall be spent
When theirs are dry, for Romeo's banishment.
Take up those cords. Poor ropes, you are beguiled,
Both you and I, for Romeo is exiled.
He made you for a highway to my bed,
135  But I, a maid, die maiden-widowed.
Come, cords, come, Nurse, I'll to my wedding bed,
And death, not Romeo take my maidenhead.

**Nurse**   Hie to your chamber. I'll find Romeo
To comfort you. I wot well where he is.
140  Hark ye, your Romeo will be here at night.
I'll to him. He is hid at Lawrence' cell.

**Juliet**   O find him, give this ring to my true knight
And bid him come to take his last farewell.

[*Exeunt*]

Tybalt's death with 'Romeo is banished'! In saying that, everyone's killed: father, mother, Tybalt, Romeo, and Juliet, all dead. 'Romeo is banished!' There's no end, no limit, no measurement, no boundary, to the death that word implies. No words can describe that sorrow. Where are my father, and my mother, Nurse?

**Nurse**   Weeping and wailing over Tybalt's corpse. Do you want to join them? Shall I take you there?

**Juliet**   Are they crying over him? My tears will flow when theirs have dried, for Romeo's banishment! Pick up the ladder. Poor ropes! You've been cheated! Both of us have, because Romeo is exiled. He made you as a route to reach my bed: but, virgin that I am, I'll die a virgin-widow. Come, ropes. Come, Nurse. I'll go to my wedding bed. Death will take my virginity: not Romeo.

**Nurse**   Go to your bedroom. I'll find Romeo to comfort you. I know exactly where he is. Listen: your Romeo will be here tonight. I'll go to him. He's hiding at Friar Lawrence's cell.

**Juliet**   Oh, do find him! [*She slips a ring from her finger*] Give this ring to my beloved, and ask him to come and take his final farewell.

[*They go*]

## Scene 3

*Friar Lawrence's cell. Enter* **Friar Lawrence**

**Friar Lawrence**    Romeo, come forth, come forth, thou fearful
man.
Affliction is enamoured of thy parts
And thou art wedded to calamity.

[*Enter* **Romeo**]

5 **Romeo**    Father, what news? What is the Prince's doom?
What sorrow craves acquaintance at my hand
That I yet know not?

**Friar Lawrence**            Too familiar
Is my dear son with such sour company.
I bring thee tidings of the Prince's doom.

10 **Romeo**    What less than doomsday is the Prince's doom?

**Friar Lawrence**    A gentler judgement vanished from his lips:
Not body's death but body's banishment.

**Romeo**    Ha! Banishment! Be merciful, say 'death'.
For exile hath more terror in his look,
15    Much more than death. Do not say 'banishment'.

**Friar Lawrence**    Hence from Verona art thou banished.
Be patient, for the world is broad and wide.

**Romeo**    There is no world without Verona walls
But purgatory, torture, hell itself;
20    Hence 'banished' is banished from the world,
And world's exile is death. Then 'banished'
Is death, mistermed. Calling death 'banished'
Thou cut'st my head off with a golden axe
And smilest upon the stroke that murders me.

## Scene 3

*Friar Lawrence's cell.* **Friar Lawrence** *enters*

**Friar Lawrence**   Romeo, come out: come out, you frightened fellow. Trouble has taken a fancy to you: you're married to misfortune!

[**Romeo** *comes from his hiding place*]

**Romeo**   What news? What's the Prince's judgement? What's the newest misfortune waiting to make my acquaintance?

**Friar Lawrence**   My dear son is becoming too familiar with such disagreeable companions. I bring news of the Prince's verdict.

**Romeo**   How far short of death is it?

**Friar Lawrence**   Leniently shorter: not death, but banishment.

**Romeo**   [*aghast*] What! Banishment? Be merciful, say 'death'. Exile is more frightening, much more, than death. Don't say 'banishment'.

**Friar Lawrence**   You are banished from Verona. Be patient: the world is broad and wide.

**Romeo**   There's no world outside the walls of Verona except purgatory, torture, and hell itself. Banished means 'banished from the world'. World-exile is the same as death. 'Banished' is a misnomer for 'death'. To call death 'banished' is like cutting my head off with a golden axe, and smiling over the stroke that murders me.

25 **Friar Lawrence**    O deadly sin, O rude unthankfulness.
Thy fault our law calls death, but the kind Prince,
Taking thy part hath rushed aside the law
And turned that black word 'death' to banishment.
This is dear mercy and thou seest it not.

30 **Romeo**    'Tis torture and not mercy. Heaven is here
Where Juliet lives, and every cat and dog
And little mouse, every unworthy thing,
Live here in heaven and may look on her,
But Romeo may not. More validity,
35 More honourable state, more courtship lives
In carrion flies than Romeo. They may seize
On the white wonder of dear Juliet's hand
And steal immortal blessing from her lips,
Who, even in pure and vestal modesty
40 Still blush, as thinking their won kisses sin.
But Romeo may not, he is banished.
Flies may do this, but I from this must fly.
They are free men but I am banished.
And say'st thou yet that exile is not death?
45 Hadst thou no poison mixed, no sharp-ground knife,
No sudden mean of death, though ne'er so mean,
But 'banished' to kill me? 'Banished'?
O Friar, the damned use that word in hell.
Howling attends it. How hast thou the heart,
50 Being a divine, a ghostly confessor,
A sin-absolver, and my friend professed,
To mangle me with that word 'banished'?

**Friar Lawrence**    Thou fond mad man, hear me a little speak.

**Romeo**    O, thou wilt speak again of banishment.

55 **Friar Lawrence**    I'll give thee armour to keep off that word,
Adversity's sweet milk, philosophy,
To comfort thee though thou art banished.

**Friar Lawrence**   Oh, what a deadly sin! Oh, crude ingratitude!
By law, it's the death penalty for what you've done, but the
kind Prince, favouring you, has set the law aside and turned
that black word 'death' to 'banishment'. This is gracious
mercy, though you don't see it.

**Romeo**   It's torture, not mercy. Heaven is here where Juliet
lives. Every cat and dog and little mouse, and and every
worthless creature live here in heaven, and can look at her. But
Romeo can't. There's more value, more honourable status,
more courteousness, in blowflies than in Romeo. They can
land upon the whiteness of dear Juliet's hand. Or steal a
divine kiss from her lips, which still blush with virginal
modesty at the thought that they commit a sin whenever they
touch each other. But Romeo cannot. He is banished. Flies can
do this, but I must fly away. They are free, but I am banished.
And do you still say that exile isn't death? Haven't you any
poison ready, or razor-edged knife, no quick way to die,
however ignoble – other than 'banished' to execute me?
Banished! Oh, Friar! The damned use that word in hell. It's a
word to be howled at. How could you have the heart, being a
priest, a confessor, one who forgives sins, and my so-called
friend, to tear me to pieces with that word 'banished'?

**Friar Lawrence**   You poor, foolish man! Listen to me a moment.

**Romeo**   Oh, you'll just say more about banishment.

**Friar Lawrence**   I'll give you a defence against the word:
consolation in adversity, an attitude of mind, which will be of
comfort to you, though you're banished.

**Romeo**    Yet 'banished'? Hang up philosophy.
Unless philosophy can make a Juliet,
60    Displant a town, reverse a Prince's doom,
It helps not, it prevails not. Talk no more.

**Friar Lawrence**    O, then I see that mad men have no ears.

**Romeo**    How should they when that wise men have no eyes?

**Friar Lawrence**    Let me dispute with thee of thy estate.

65    **Romeo**    Thou canst not speak of that thou dost not feel.
Wert thou as young as I, Juliet thy love,
An hour but married, Tybalt murdered,
Doting like me, and like me banished,
Then mightst thou speak, then mightst thou tear thy hair
70    And fall upon the ground as I do now,
Taking the measure of an unmade grave.

[*Knock*]

**Friar Lawrence**    Arise, one knocks. Good Romeo, hide
thyself.

**Romeo**    Not I, unless the breath of heartsick groans
75    Mist-like infold me from the search of eyes.

[*Knock*]

**Friar Lawrence**    Hark how they knock! Who's there? Romeo,
arise,
Thou wilt be taken! Stay awhile! Stand up!

[*Knock*]

Run to my study! By and by! God's will,
80    What simpleness is this? I come, I come!

**Romeo**   Still on about 'banished'? Unless an 'attitude of mind' can make a Juliet, transplant a town, reverse a Prince's sentence, it's no help, no benefit – so say no more.

**Friar Lawrence**   Oh, then I take it that madmen have no ears.

**Romeo**   Why should they, when wise men have no eyes?

**Friar Lawrence**   Let me discuss your situation with you.

**Romeo**   You can't talk about what you don't feel. If you were my age, and Juliet your loved one, married just one hour, Tybalt murdered, deeply in love like me, and like me banished, then you could speak! Then you could tear your hair, and fall on the ground as I do now, measuring out my length for a future grave!

[*He flings himself to the floor. A knocking is heard at the door*]

**Friar Lawrence**   Get up. Someone's knocking. Good Romeo, hide yourself.

**Romeo**   I won't – unless I'm hidden by the mist made by my heartsick groans!

[*The knocking continues*]

**Friar Lawrence**   Listen to them knocking! Who's there? Romeo, get up! You'll be caught! [*He calls*] Hold on a moment! [*To* **Romeo**] Stand up – run to my study! [*He calls*] In a minute! [*To* **Romeo**] God's will! What stupidity is this? [*He calls again*] I'm

[*Knock*]

Who knocks so hard? Whence come you, what's your will?

**Nurse**  [*Within*] Let me come in and you shall know my
errand. I come from Lady Juliet.

**Friar Lawrence**              Welcome then.

[*Enter* **Nurse**]

**Nurse**  O holy Friar, O, tell me, holy Friar,
85    Where is my lady's lord, where's Romeo?

**Friar Lawrence**  There on the ground, with his own tears
made drunk.

**Nurse**  O, he is even in my mistress' case.
Just in her case. O woeful sympathy,
90    Piteous predicament. Even so lies she,
Blubbering and weeping, weeping and blubbering.
Stand up, stand up! Stand, and you be a man!
For Juliet's sake, for her sake, rise and stand!
Why should you fall into so deep an O?

[*He rises*]

**Romeo**  Nurse.

95 **Nurse**              Ah sir, ah sir, death's the end of all.

**Romeo**  Spak'st thou of Juliet? How is it with her?
Doth not she think me an old murderer
Now I have stained the childhood of our joy
With blood removed but little from her own?
100    Where is she? And how doth she? And what says
My concealed lady to our cancelled love?

coming, I'm coming! [*The knock is louder now*] Who's knocking so loudly? Where have you come from? What do you want?

**Nurse**    [*outside*] Let me come in, and I'll tell you. I come from the Lady Juliet.

**Friar Lawrence**    [*opening the door*] Welcome, then.

**Nurse**    [*dashing in*] Oh, holy Friar! Oh, tell me, holy Friar – where's my lady's husband? Where's Romeo?

**Friar Lawrence**    There on the ground, drunk with his own tears.

**Nurse**    Oh, he's in the same state as my mistress. Just the same. Oh, what sympathy in sorrow! What a pitiful affair! She lies just the same – blubbering and weeping, weeping and blubbering. [*To* **Romeo**] Stand up, stand up! Stand, if you're a man! For Juliet's sake, for her sake, rise and stand! Why should you slip into so deep a hole?

**Romeo**    [*getting up*] Nurse!

**Nurse**    [*with misplaced words of comfort*] Ah, sir; ah, sir! Death comes to all things in the end!

**Romeo**    Did you speak of Juliet? How is she? Does she think I'm an habitual murderer, now that I've ruined the early days of our bliss with the blood of her near relative? Where is she? How is she? What does my secret wife say about our separation?

**Nurse**   O she says nothing, sir, but weeps and weeps,
And now falls on her bed, and then starts up,
And Tybalt calls, and then on Romeo cries,
And then down falls again.

105 **Romeo**                                As if that name,
Shot from the deadly level of a gun,
Did murder her, as that name's cursed hand
Murdered her kinsman. O, tell me, Friar, tell me,
In what vile part of this anatomy
110 Doth my name lodge? Tell me that I may sack
The hateful mansion!

**Friar Lawrence**            Hold thy desperate hand.
Art thou a man? Thy form cries out thou art.
Thy tears are womanish, thy wild acts denote
The unreasonable fury of a beast.
115 Unseemly woman in a seeming man,
And ill-beseeming beast in seeming both!
Thou hast amazed me. By my holy order,
I thought thy disposition better tempered.
Hast thou slain Tybalt? Wilt thou slay thyself?
120 And slay thy lady that in thy life lives,
By doing damned hate upon thyself?
Why rail'st thou on thy birth, the heaven and earth?
Since birth, and heaven, and earth all three do meet
In thee at once; which thou at once would lose.
125 Fie, fie, thou sham'st thy shape, thy love, thy wit,
Which, like a usurer, abound'st in all,
And usest none in that true use indeed
Which should bedeck thy shape, thy love, thy wit.
Thy noble shape is but a form of wax
130 Digressing from the valour of a man;
Thy dear love sworn but hollow perjury,
Killing that love which thou hast vowed to cherish;
Thy wit, that ornament to shape and love,

**Nurse**   Oh, she says nothing, sir; just weeps and weeps. One moment she falls on her bed, then gets up, calls out 'Tybalt', and then cries out 'Romeo', and then falls down again.

**Romeo**   It is as if my name, shot from the muzzle of a gun, had murdered her as the hand of that cursed name murdered her cousin! Oh, tell me Friar, tell me, in what vile part of my body does my name lie? Tell me, so that I can attack the hated place! [*He draws his dagger to stab himself, but the* **Nurse** *snatches it from him*]

**Friar Lawrence**   Restrain yourself! Do you call yourself a man? By shape you are, but your tears are womanish, and your wild behaviour suggests the unreasoning fury of a beast! Man though you seem, you're behaving like an unseemly woman: the two put together make a very repulsive animal! You have amazed me. By my faith, I thought your character was better balanced. So you've killed Tybalt? Will you now kill yourself? And kill your wife, whose life is one with yours, by damning your immortal soul with suicide? Why do you rant on about your birth, and heaven, and earth, when all three – birth, heaven and earth – are combined in you, and would therefore all be lost together? Come, come! You disgrace your human body, your love, your intelligence! Like a moneylender, you have plenty of assets, but you don't use them properly to improve your body, your love or your intelligence! Your noble body is merely a waxwork figure, lacking manliness. Your vows of love are simply empty lies, killing the love that you promised to cherish. Your intelligence, that adornment of the body and of love, is misguided in the advice it gives them

165

Misshapen in the conduct of them both,
135 Like powder in a skilless soldier's flask
Is set afire by thine own ignorance,
And thou dismembered with thine own defence.
What, rouse thee, man! Thy Juliet is alive,
For whose dear sake thou wast but lately dead.
140 There art thou happy. Tybalt would kill thee,
But thou slew'st Tybalt. There art thou happy.
The law that threatened death becomes thy friend
And turns it to exile. There art thou happy.
A pack of blessings light upon thy back;
145 Happiness courts thee in her best array;
But like a misbehaved and sullen wench
Thou pouts upon thy fortune and thy love.
Take heed, take heed, for such die miserable.
Go, get thee to thy love, as was decreed,
150 Ascend her chamber; hence, and comfort her.
But look thou stay not till the watch be set,
For then thou can'st not pass to Mantua,
Where thou shalt live till we can find a time
To blaze your marriage, reconcile your friends,
155 Beg pardon of the Prince, and call thee back
With twenty hundred thousand times more joy
Than thou went'st forth in lamentation.
Go before, Nurse. Commend me to thy lady,
And bid her hasten all the house to bed,
160 Which heavy sorrow makes them apt unto.
Romeo is coming.

**Nurse**   O Lord, I could have stayed here all the night
To hear good counsel. O what learning is!
My lord, I'll tell my lady you will come.

165 **Romeo**   Do so, and bid my sweet prepare to chide.

**Nurse**   Here, sir, a ring she bid me give you, sir.
Hie you, make haste, for it grows very late.

both, and is like gunpowder in an untrained soldier's powder-flask, touched off by ignorance, blowing you apart with what should be defending you. What? Stir yourself, man! Your Juliet is alive, for whose dear sake just now you wanted to be dead. That's good reason to be happy. Tybalt would have killed you, but you killed Tybalt. Another reason for happiness. The law that threatened you with death becomes your friend, and substitutes exile: in that you are happy, too. You've had a parcel of blessings descend upon you. Happiness has favoured you in attractive ways, but like a badly behaved and sullen wench, you've pouted at your good fortune and your love. Take heed, take heed: such people die miserable. Go, and proceed to your loved-one as was planned. Climb into her room. Be off, and comfort her. But mind you don't stay till the night guards start their shift! Then, you couldn't leave for Mantua, where you shall live till the time is right for us to make your marriage public, reconcile your friends, beg pardon of the Prince, and call you back with two million times more joy than when you left in tears. Go ahead, Nurse. My regards to your lady, and tell her to encourage everyone to go to bed early, which heavy sorrow makes them ready for. Romeo is coming.

**Nurse**   Oh lord, I could have stayed here all night listening to such good advice. Oh, what education is! My lord, I'll tell my lady you are coming.

**Romeo**   Please do, and tell my sweet one to get ready to scold me.

**Nurse**   Here's a ring, sir, that she asked me to give you, sir. Hurry. Make haste. It's getting very late.

**Romeo**    How well my comfort is revived by this.

**Friar Lawrence**    Go hence, good night, and here stands all
170      your state:
Either be gone before the Watch be set,
Or by the break of day disguised from hence.
Sojourn in Mantua. I'll find out your man,
And he shall signify from time to time
175      Every good hap to you that chances here.
Give me thy hand. 'Tis late. Farewell. Good night.

**Romeo**    But that a joy past joy calls out on me,
It were a grief so brief to part with thee.
Farewell.

[*Exeunt*]

## Scene 4

*Capulet's house. Enter* **Capulet, Lady Capulet** *and* **Paris**

**Capulet**    Things have fallen out, sir, so unluckily
That we have had no time to move our daughter.
Look you, she loved her kinsman Tybalt dearly,
And so did I. Well, we were born to die.
5      'Tis very late. She'll not come down tonight.
I promise you, but for your company,
I would have been abed an hour ago.

**Paris**    These times of woe afford no times to woo.
Madam, good night. Commend me to your daughter.

10  **Lady Capulet**    I will, and know her mind early tomorrow.
Tonight she's mewed up to her heaviness.

**Romeo**   How much better I feel now!

**Friar Lawrence**   Off you go. Good night!

[*The* **Nurse** *leaves*]

Your whole future depends on this: either be gone before the guard goes on duty, or by daybreak, leaving here disguised. Stay in Mantua. I'll find your servant, and from time to time he'll pass on each bit of good news as it happens here. Give me your hand. It's late. Farewell. Good night!

**Romeo**   If I hadn't been summoned by a source of joy greater than joy itself, I'd be sad at parting from you so abruptly. Farewell!

[*He runs off and* **Friar Lawrence** *returns to his cell*]

## Scene 4

*Capulet's house. Enter* **Capulet, Lady Capulet** *and* **Paris**

**Capulet**   Things have happened so unluckily, sir, that we haven't had time to broach matters with our daughter. You see, she loved her cousin Tybalt dearly, and so did I. Well, we were born to die! It's very late. She'll not come down tonight. I assure you, but for your company, I'd have been in bed an hour ago.

**Paris**   Times of grief aren't proper times for courtship. Madam, good night. Give my compliments to your daughter.

**Lady Capulet**   I will, and I'll know her mind by early tomorrow. Tonight she's shut up with her sorrows.

[**Paris** *offers to go in and* **Capulet** *calls him again*]

**Capulet**    Sir Paris, I will make a desperate tender
    Of my child's love. I think she will be ruled
    In all respects by me; nay, more, I doubt it not.
15   Wife, go you to her ere you go to bed,
    Acquaint her here of my son Paris' love,
    And bid her – mark you me? – on Wednesday next –
    But soft – what day is this?

**Paris**               Monday, my lord.

**Capulet**    Monday! Ha ha! Well, Wednesday is too soon.
20   A Thursday let it be, a Thursday, tell her,
    She shall be married to this noble earl.
    Will you be ready? Do you like this haste?
    We'll keep no great ado – a friend or two.
    For, hark you, Tybalt being slain so late,
25   It may be thought we held him carelessly,
    Being our kinsman, if we revel much.
    Therefore we'll have some half a dozen friends
    And there an end. But what say you to Thursday?

**Paris**    My lord, I would that Thursday were tomorrow.

30 **Capulet**    Well, get you gone. A Thursday be it then.
    Go you to Juliet ere you go to bed,
    Prepare her, wife, against this wedding day.
    Farewell, my lord. Light to my chamber, ho!
    Afore me, it is so very late that we
35   May call it early by and by. Good night.

[*Exeunt*]

[**Paris** *starts to leave, but* **Capulet** *calls him back*]

**Capulet**   Sir Paris! I'll make so bold as to offer you my child's love. I think she'll be ruled by me in all respects; nay more, have no doubt about it. Wife, go to her before you go to bed. Tell her of young Paris's love, and tell her – note this – that next Wednesday . . . Hold on – what day is it today?

**Paris**   Monday, my lord.

**Capulet**   Monday! Ah, yes! Well, Wednesday is too soon. Let's say Thursday: on Thursday, tell her, she'll be married to this noble earl. Will you be ready? Do you approve of the quick action? We won't make it a big affair: a friend or two, because, you know, Tybalt being killed so recently, people might think we took it too lightly, Tybalt being our relative, if we make too much of a fuss. Therefore we'll just have half a dozen friends and leave it at that. [*To* **Paris**] What do you say to Thursday?

**Paris**   My lord, I wish Thursday were tomorrow.

**Capulet**   Well, be off with you then. On Thursday let it be. [*To* **Lady Capulet**] Go to Juliet before you go to bed. Prepare her, wife, with this wedding day in mind. Farewell, my lord. [*To his* **Servant**] Put lights in my bedroom, there! Believe me, it's so very late we'll soon be calling it early! Good night!

[*They all leave*]

## Scene 5

*Juliet's bedroom.* **Romeo** *and* **Juliet** *stand at the window*

**Juliet**    Wilt thou be gone? It is not yet near day.
It was the nightingale and not the lark
That pierced the fearful hollow of thine ear.
Nightly she sings on yond pomegranate tree.
5    Believe me, love, it was the nightingale.

**Romeo**    It was the lark, the herald of the morn,
No nightingale. Look, love, what envious streaks
Do lace the severing clouds in yonder east.
Night's candles are burnt out, and jocund day
10    Stands tiptoe on the misty mountain tops.
I must be gone and live, or stay and die.

**Juliet**    Yond light is not daylight, I know it, I.
It is some meteor that the sun exhales
To be to thee this night a torchbearer
15    And light thee on thy way to Mantua.
Therefore stay yet: thou need'st not to be gone.

**Romeo**    Let me be ta'en, let me be put to death.
I am content, so thou wilt have it so.
I'll say yon grey is not the morning's eye,
20    'Tis but the pale reflex of Cynthia's brow.
Nor that is not the lark whose notes do beat
The vaulty heaven so high above our heads.
I have more care to stay than will to go.
Come death, and welcome. Juliet wills it so.
25    How is't, my soul? Let's talk. It is not day.

**Juliet**    It is, it is. Hie hence, begone, away.
It is the lark that sings so out of tune,
Straining harsh discords and unpleasing sharps.
Some say the lark makes sweet division.

## Scene 5

*Juliet's bedroom.* **Romeo** *and* **Juliet** *stand at the window*

**Juliet**  Must you go? It's not nearly day. It was the nightingale
and not the lark your worried ear could hear. She sings every
night on that pomegranate tree there. Believe me, love, it was
the nightingale!

**Romeo**  It was the lark, morning's herald, not the nightingale.
Look, my love, how jealous daylight pierces through the
clouds, there in the east. The stars have disappeared, and a
pleasant day stands poised on the misty mountain tops. I
must be gone, and live – or stay and die.

**Juliet**  That light's not daylight! I know it! It's some meteor of
the sun's, which is to be your torchbearer tonight, to light your
way to Mantua. Therefore, stay a little longer. You don't have
to go yet.

**Romeo**  Let me be arrested. Let me be put to death! That's all
right with me if it's what you want. I'll say that the grey light
over there is not a sign of morning: it's just the moon's
reflection; and that it's not the lark whose song reaches for the
sky above our heads. I'd much prefer to stay than to go. Come,
death, and welcome! Juliet so wishes it. Soul, how are you?
[*Taking* **Juliet** *by the arm and turning back into the room*] Let's
talk. It isn't day.

**Juliet**  [*panicked*] It is! It is! Go now! Be gone! Go! It was the
lark's singing so out of tune, with its harsh discords and shrill
notes . . . Some say the lark makes intertwining chords: this

30    This doth not so, for she divideth us.
      Some say the lark and loathed toad change eyes.
      O, now I would they had changed voices too,
      Since arm from arm that voice doth us affray,
      Hunting thee hence with hunt's-up to the day.
35    O now be gone, more light and light it grows.

**Romeo**    More light and light: more dark and dark our woes.

[*Enter* **Nurse** *hastily*]

**Nurse**    Madam.

**Juliet**    Nurse?

**Nurse**    Your lady mother is coming to your chamber.
40    The day is broke, be wary, look about.

[*Exit*]

**Juliet**    Then, window, let day in and let life out.

**Romeo**    Farewell, farewell. One kiss and I'll descend.

[*He goes down*]

**Juliet**    Art thou gone so? Love, lord, ay husband, friend,
      I must hear from thee every day in the hour,
45    For in a minute there are many days.
      O, by this count I shall be much in years
      Ere I again behold my Romeo.

**Romeo**    Farewell.
      I will omit no opportunity
50    That may convey my greetings, love, to thee.

**Juliet**    O think'st thou we shall ever meet again?

one doesn't – she separates us. Some say the lark exchanged eyes with the loathsome toad: I wish now they'd changed voices, too. The lark's voice parts us, chasing you away with a huntsman's early morning call. Go now. It's getting so much lighter.

**Romeo**    Much lighter our light: much darker our sorrows.

[*The* **Nurse** *enters in haste*]

**Nurse**    Madam!

**Juliet**    Nurse?

**Nurse**    Your mother is coming to your bedroom. It's daybreak. On your guard: be careful!

[*The* **Nurse** *hurries out*]

**Juliet**    So then, window: let daylight in, and let life out.

**Romeo**    Goodbye. Goodbye. One kiss, and I'll climb down.

[*They embrace and* **Romeo** *descends*]

**Juliet**    Have you gone – love, lord, yes, husband, lover? I must hear from you every day by the hour. Every minute contains so many days. By that calculation I'll be much older when I next see my Romeo.

**Romeo**    [*from below*] Farewell! I'll miss no chance to send my greetings to you, dearest.

**Juliet**    Oh, do you think we'll ever meet again?

**Romeo**   I doubt it not, and all these woes shall serve
For sweet discourses in our times to come.

**Juliet**   O God, I have an ill-divining soul!
55   Methinks I see thee, now thou art so low,
As one dead in the bottom of a tomb.
Either my eyesight fails, or thou look'st pale.

**Romeo**   And trust me, love, in my eye so do you.
Dry sorrow drinks our blood. Adieu, adieu.

[*Exit*]

60 **Juliet**   O Fortune, Fortune! All men call thee fickle;
If thou art fickle, what dost thou with him
That is renowned for faith? Be fickle, Fortune,
For then I hope thou wilt not keep him long,
But send him back.

[*Enter* **Lady Capulet**]

65 **Lady Capulet**          Ho, daughter, are you up?

**Juliet**   Who is't that calls? It is my lady mother.
Is she not down so late, or up so early?
What unaccustomed cause procures her hither?

[*She goes down from the window*]

**Lady Capulet**   Why, how now Juliet?

**Juliet**                              Madam, I am not well.

**Lady Capulet**   Evermore weeping for your cousin's death?
70   What, wilt thou wash him from his grave with tears?
And if thou couldst, thou couldst not make him live.
Therefore have done. Some grief shows much of love,
But much of grief shows still some want of wit.

**Romeo**    I have no doubt. All these sorrows will make lovely reminiscences in time to come.

**Juliet**    Oh God! I have a presentiment of evil: I seem to see you – now you're down below – as if you're at the bottom of a tomb. Either my eyesight's failing, or you look pale.

**Romeo**    Believe me, in my eyes you do too. Sighs drain the heart of its blood. Adieu! Adieu!

[**Romeo** *leaves*]

**Juliet**    Oh Fortune, Fortune! All men call you fickle! If you are so fickle, why have dealings with one like Romeo, renowned for his faith? Be fickle, Fortune! because then you will not keep him long, but send him back to me.

**Lady Capulet**    [*outside*] Daughter! Are you up?

**Juliet**    Who's that calling? It's my mother. Is she late to bed, or an early riser? What's happened to bring her here? [*She hides her face in her pillow*]

[*Enter* **Lady Capulet**]

**Lady Capulet**    What's the matter, Juliet?

**Juliet**    Madam, I'm not well.

**Lady Capulet**    [*misunderstanding*] Still weeping for your cousin's death? What, will you wash him from his grave with your tears? Even if you could, it wouldn't bring him back to life. Therefore, cry no more. Grief in moderation is a clear sign of love. Too much of it is foolishness.

**Juliet**    Yet let me weep for such a feeling loss.

75  **Lady Capulet**    So shall you feel the loss but not the friend
Which you weep for.

**Juliet**                                   Feeling so the loss,
I cannot choose but ever weep the friend.

**Lady Capulet**    Well, girl, thou weepst not so much for his death
As that the villain lives which slaughtered him.

**Juliet**    What villain, madam?

80  **Lady Capulet**                              That same villain Romeo.

**Juliet**    Villain and he be many miles asunder.
God pardon him. I do with all my heart.
And yet no man like he doth grieve my heart.

**Lady Capulet**    That is because the traitor murderer lives.

85  **Juliet**    Ay madam, from the reach of these my hands.
Would none but I might venge my cousin's death.

**Lady Capulet**    We will have vengeance for it, fear thou not.
Then weep no more. I'll send to one in Mantua,
Where that same banished runagate doth live,
90  Shall give him such an unaccustomed dram
That he shall soon keep Tybalt company;
And then I hope thou wilt be satisfied.

**Juliet**    Indeed I never shall be satisfied
With Romeo, till I behold him – dead –
95  Is my poor heart so for a kinsman vexed.
Madam, if you could find out but a man
To bear a poison, I would temper it –
That Romeo should upon receipt thereof
Soon sleep in quiet. O, how my heart abhors
100  To hear him named, and cannot come to him

**Juliet**    Let me cry for such a grievous loss.

**Lady Capulet**    You'll feel the loss, but that won't help the friend for whom you weep.

**Juliet**    I feel the loss so much, I can't stop weeping for the friend.

**Lady Capulet**    Well, my girl, you're weeping not so much for Tybalt's death, but rather that the villain's still alive who murdered him.

**Juliet**    What villain, madam?

**Lady Capulet**    That villain Romeo.

**Juliet**    [*to herself*] That villain's many miles off now. [*To* **Lady Capulet**] God forgive him. I do, with all my heart. Yet no man grieves my heart more than he does.

**Lady Capulet**    That's because the traitorous murderer lives.

**Juliet**    Yes, madam—beyond the reach of these hands of mine! Would that I alone could revenge my cousin's death!

**Lady Capulet**    We'll have our vengeance, do not fear. So weep no more. I'll send someone to Mantua, where that banished rogue is living, and he'll give him such an unusual cocktail that he'll soon be keeping Tybalt company. Then I trust you'll be satisfied.

**Juliet**    Indeed, I never shall be satisfied with Romeo till I behold him – dead [*she completes the sentence without pausing*] is my poor heart, I mourn my kinsman so much. [*her mother is suitably misled*] Madam, if you could find a man to transport the poison, I'd mix it so that Romeo, on receiving it, would soon sleep sweet. Oh, how my heart loathes to hear him

To wreak the love I bore my cousin
Upon his body that hath slaughtered him.

**Lady Capulet**    Find thou the means and I'll find such a man.
But now I'll tell thee joyful tidings, girl.

105 **Juliet**    And joy comes well in such a needy time.
What are they, I beseech your ladyship?

**Lady Capulet**    Well, well, thou hast a careful father, child;
One who to put thee from thy heaviness
Hath sorted out a sudden day of joy,
110    That thou expects not, nor I looked not for.

**Juliet**    Madam, in happy time. What day is that?

**Lady Capulet**    Marry, my child, early next Thursday morn
The gallant, young, and noble gentleman,
The County Paris, at Saint Peter's Church,
115    Shall happily make thee there a joyful bride.

**Juliet**    Now by Saint Peter's Church, and Peter too,
He shall not make me there a joyful bride.
I wonder at this haste, that I must wed
Ere he that should be husband comes to woo.
120    I pray you tell my lord and father, madam,
I will not marry yet. And when I do, I swear
It shall be Romeo, whom you know I hate,
Rather than Paris. These are news indeed.

**Lady Capulet**    Here comes your father, tell him so yourself,
125    And see how he will take it at your hands.

[*Enter* **Capulet** *and* **Nurse**]

**Capulet**    When the sun sets the earth doth drizzle dew,
But for the sunset of my brother's son
It rains downright.
How now, a conduit, girl? What, still in tears?

named, when I can't reach him to wreak the love that I had for my cousin on his body!

**Lady Capulet**   You find the means, and I'll find the man. But now, I've got good news for you, my girl.

**Juliet**   Good news is welcome at such a needy time. What is it, may I ask your ladyship?

**Lady Capulet**   Well, well, you have a caring father, child: one who has arranged an unexpected day of joy for you, that even surprised me, to lift you out of your sorrow.

**Juliet**   Madam, most timely! What kind of day is that?

**Lady Capulet**   Well, my child, early next Thursday morning the gallant, young and noble gentleman the Count Paris will make you a happy bride at St Peter's Church!

**Juliet**   [*resolutely*] Now by Saint Peter's Church and Peter too, he won't make me a happy bride there! I'm amazed at this haste, that I must marry before the man who's to be my husband starts to court me! With respect: tell my lord and father, madam that I will not marry yet. And when I do, I swear it will be to Romeo – whom you know I hate – rather than to Paris. News indeed! [*She pants and cries with anger*]

**Lady Capulet**   Here's your father now. Tell him so yourself, and see how he takes it.

[*Enter **Capulet** and **Nurse**. They see **Juliet** in floods of tears*]

**Capulet**   [*to **Juliet***] After sunset, dew falls. After the death of my brother's son, it pours. What's the matter, girl? Are you a down-spout? What, still crying? One continuous shower? In

130   Evermore showering? In one little body
      Thou counterfeits a bark, a sea, a wind.
      For still thy eyes, which I may call the sea,
      Do ebb and flow with tears. The bark thy body is,
      Sailing in this salt flood, the winds thy sighs,
135   Who raging with thy tears and they with them,
      Without a sudden calm will overset
      Thy tempest-tossed body. How now, wife?
      Have you delivered to her our decree?

**Lady Capulet**   Ay sir, but she will none, she gives you thanks.
140   I would the fool were married to her grave.

**Capulet**   Soft. Take me with you, take me with you, wife.
      How? Will she none? Doth she not give us thanks?
      Is she not proud? Doth she not count her blest,
      Unworthy as she is, that we have wrought
145   So worthy a gentleman to be her bride?

**Juliet**   Not proud you have, but thankful that you have.
      Proud can I never be of what I hate,
      But thankful even for hate that is meant love.

**Capulet**   How, how, how, how? Chopped logic? What is this?
150   'Proud' and 'I thank you' and 'I thank you not'
      And yet 'not proud'? Mistress minion you,
      Thank me no thankings nor proud me no prouds,
      But fettle your fine joints 'gainst Thursday next
      To go with Paris to Saint Peter's Church,
155   Or I will drag thee on a hurdle thither.
      Out, you green-sickness carrion! Out, you baggage!
      You tallow-face!

**Lady Capulet**      Fie, fie. What, are you mad?

**Juliet**   Good father, I beseech you on my knees.
      Hear me with patience but to speak a word.

one little body you resemble a ship, a sea, and a wind. Your eyes (I'll call them the sea) are ebbing and flowing with tears. Your body is the ship, sailing on the salty ocean. The winds are your sighs which, competing with your tears, and vice versa, will overturn your storm-tossed body unless there is a sudden calm! [*to* **Lady Capulet**] How about it, wife? Have you told her my decision?

**Lady Capulet**   Yes, sir – she thanks you but she'll none of it. I wish the stupid girl would marry into her grave!

**Capulet**   Hold on. I'm not with you, I'm not with you, wife. How do you mean – she'll none of it? Doesn't she thank us? Isn't she proud? Doesn't she think herself fortunate, unworthy as she is, that we've persuaded such a worthy gentleman to be her bridegroom?

**Juliet**   I'm not proud that you have, though I'm grateful that you have. I can never be proud of what I hate. But I'm grateful inasmuch as what I hate, you intended me to love.

**Capulet**   What, what! What, what! Subtle hair-splitting! What's this? 'Proud', and 'Thank you', and 'No, thanks' – and even 'Not proud'. You cheeky girl, you, I'll have none of your 'thanks', thank you, none of your 'prouds'! Just get your fine self ready for next Thursday, to go with Paris to Saint Peter's Church, or I'll drag you there on a sledge! Pah! You vomity-looking object! Get away with you, you minx! You lardy-face!

**Lady Capulet**   [*trying to calm her husband down*] Oh, really, really! Have you lost your senses?

**Juliet**   [*falling before him*] Dear father, I beg you on my knees: have patience while I say one word –

160 **Capulet**   Hang thee young baggage, disobedient wretch!
       I tell thee what – get thee to church a Thursday
       Or never after look me in the face.
       Speak not, reply not, do not answer me.
       My fingers itch. Wife, we scarce thought us blest
165    That God had lent us but this only child;
       But now I see this one is one too much,
       And that we have a curse in having her.
       Out on her, hilding.

   **Nurse**                    God in heaven bless her.
       You are to blame, my lord, to rate her so.

170 **Capulet**   And why, my Lady Wisdom? Hold your tongue,
       Good Prudence! Smatter with your gossips, go.

   **Nurse**   I speak no treason.

   **Capulet**                    O God 'i' good e'en!

   **Nurse**   May not one speak?

   **Capulet**                    Peace, you mumbling fool!
       Utter your gravity o'er a gossip's bowl,
       For here we need it not.

175 **Lady Capulet**             You are too hot.

   **Capulet**   God's bread, it makes me mad! Day, night, work,
          play,
       Alone, in company, still my care hath been
       To have her matched. And having now provided
180    A gentleman of noble parentage,
       Of fair demesnes, youthful and nobly ligned,
       Stuffed, as they say, with honourable parts,
       Proportioned as one's thought would wish a man –
       And then to have a wretched puling fool,
185    A whining mammet, in her fortune's tender,
       To answer 'I'll not wed, I cannot love,

184

**Capulet**   Be hanged to you, you hussy, you disobedient wretch! I'll tell you what: get you to church on Thursday, or never look me in the face again. Don't say anything! Don't reply! Don't answer me back! My fingers are itching! Wife, we thought we were very lucky that God gave us this only child — but now I realize this one is one too many, and that we've been cursed in having her! To blazes with her, the slut!

**Nurse**   God in heaven bless her! You're to blame, my lord, for shouting at her like that!

**Capulet**   And why did I, Lady Knowall? Hold your tongue, Clever Pru! Go and natter with your cronies!

**Nurse**   I'm not being disloyal —

**Capulet**   [*pointing to the door*] Good night to you!

**Nurse**   Can't a body speak?

**Capulet**   Shut up, you mumbling fool! Preach your sermon over your gossipy porridge-bowls. We can do without it here!

**Lady Capulet**   You are too worked up!

**Capulet**   God's holy bread! It makes me mad. Day and night, hour by hour, at work, at play, alone, in company, it's been my one concern to find her a husband. And now I've provided a gentleman from a noble family, of good appearance, youthful, well brought up — 'really decent' as they say, a handsome figure of a man, only to have a wretched, puking idiot, a whining cry-baby, when good fortune is offered to her, reply 'I won't marry, I can't love, I'm too young, please excuse me'! Be

I am too young, I pray you pardon me!'
But, and you will not wed, I'll pardon you!
Graze where you will, you shall not house with me.
190   Look to't, think on't, I do not use to jest.
Thursday is near. Lay hand on heart. Advise.
And you be mine I'll give you to my friend;
And you be not, hang! Beg! Starve! Die in the streets!
For by my soul I'll ne'er acknowledge thee,
195   Nor what is mine shall never do thee good.
Trust to't, bethink you. I'll not be forsworn.

[*Exit*]

**Juliet**    Is there no pity sitting in the clouds
That sees into the bottom of my grief?
O sweet my mother, cast me not away,
200   Delay this marriage for a month, a week,
Or if you do not, make the bridal bed
In that dim monument where Tybalt lies.

**Lady Capulet**    Talk not to me, for I'll not speak a word.
Do as thou wilt, for I have done with thee.

[*Exit*]

205   **Juliet**    O God, O Nurse, how shall this be prevented?
My husband is on earth, my faith in heaven.
How shall that faith return again to earth
Unless that husband send it me from heaven
By leaving earth? Comfort me, counsel me.
210   Alack, alack, that heaven should practise stratagems
Upon so soft a subject as myself.
What sayst thou? Hast thou not a word of joy?
Some comfort, Nurse.

**Nurse**                          Faith, here it is.
Romeo is banished, and all the world to nothing

obstinate about marrying and I'll 'pardon' you! Get your fodder where you can, you won't live in my house! See about it. Think about it. It's not my habit to joke. Thursday is close. Think hard about it. Consider it. If you're a daughter of mine, I'll give you to my friend. If not you can hang, beg, starve, die in the streets, for by my soul I'll never recognize you, or leave you anything in my will! You can be sure of that. So think about it. I won't change my mind!

[**Capulet** *storms out*]

**Juliet**    Has God no pity for me, in the depths of my grief! Dearest mother, don't cast me off! Postpone the marriage for a month, a week, or, if you don't, prepare a bridal bed in the tomb where Tybalt lies!

**Lady Capulet**    Don't talk to me. I'm not saying a word. Do as you wish. I've done with you.

[*She leaves in a mighty huff*]

**Juliet**    Oh God! Oh Nurse! How can this be stopped? My husband is alive: my vows registered in heaven. How can I recover them unless my husband dies? Comfort me. Advise me. Alas, alas, that heaven should play its tricks upon so weak a person as myself! What do you say? Have you no cheery word? Some comfort, Nurse?

**Nurse**    Indeed, here it is: Romeo is banished. It's a safe bet that

215    That he dares ne'er come back to challenge you.
      Or if he do, it needs must be by stealth.
      Then, since the case so stands as now it doth,
      I think it best you married with the County.
      O, he's a lovely gentleman.
220    Romeo's a dishclout to him. An eagle, madam,
      Hath not so green, so quick, so fair an eye
      As Paris hath. Beshrew my very heart,
      I think you are happy in this second match,
      For it excels your first; or, if it did not,
225    Your first is dead, or 'twere as good he were
      As living here and you no use of him.

**Juliet**    Speakest thou from thy heart?

**Nurse**    And from my soul too, else beshrew them both.

**Juliet**    Amen.

230 **Nurse**   What?

**Juliet**    Well, thou hast comforted me marvellous much.
      Go in, and tell my lady I am gone,
      Having displeased my father, to Lawrence' cell,
      To make confession and to be absolved.

235 **Nurse**   Marry, I will; and this is wisely done.

                                   [*Exit*]

**Juliet**    Ancient damnation! O most wicked fiend,
      Is it more sin to wish me thus forsworn,
      Or to dispraise my lord with that same tongue
      Which she hath praised him with above compare
      So many thousand times? Go, counsellor.
240    Thou and my bosom henceforth shall be twain.
      I'll to the Friar to know his remedy.
      If all else fail, myself have power to die.

                                   [*Exit*]

he'll never dare to return to claim you as his: or if he does he'll have to do it secretly. Since things are as they are, I think you'd be best to marry Count Paris. Oh, he's a lovely gentleman! Romeo's a dishcloth compared with him! An eagle hasn't eyes so green, so quick, so attractive as those of Paris. Damn me if I'm wrong: I think this second marriage is very fortunate, because it's better than your first. Even if it wasn't, your first husband's dead, or as good as, him being alive but you having no contact with him.

**Juliet**   Is this in all sincerity, from your heart?

**Nurse**   And from my soul, too. Curse them both, otherwise.

**Juliet**   Amen to that!

**Nurse**   What?

**Juliet**   Well, you've been a real comfort. Go and tell my mother that, having upset my father, I've gone to Friar Lawrence, to make confession and be absolved.

**Nurse**   Indeed I will. This is very sensible.

[*The* **Nurse** *goes*]

**Juliet**   You old devil! You wicked fiend! Which is more sinful: to tempt me to break my marriage vows, or to belittle my husband with the same tongue with which so many times before she praised him beyond all compare? Go, my adviser: you'll share none of my secrets from now on. I'll go to the Friar, to see what he can recommend. If all else fails, I'll kill myself.

[**Juliet** *goes*]

# Act four

## Scene 1

*Friar Lawrence's cell. Enter* **Friar Lawrence** *and* **Paris**


**Friar Lawrence**    On Thursday, sir? The time is very short.

**Paris**    My father Capulet will have it so,
And I am nothing slow to slack his haste.

**Friar Lawrence**    You say you do not know the lady's mind.
5    Uneven is the course. I like it not.

**Paris**    Immoderately she weeps for Tybalt's death,
And therefore have I little talked of love,
For Venus smiles not in a house of tears.
Now sir, her father counts it dangerous
10    That she do give her sorrow so much sway,
And in his wisdom hastes our marriage
To stop the inundation of her tears
Which, too much minded by herself alone,
May be put from her by society.
15    Now do you know the reason of this haste.

**Friar Lawrence**    I would I knew not why it should be slowed.
Look sir, here comes the lady toward my cell.

[*Enter* **Juliet**]

**Paris**    Happily met, my lady and my wife.

**Juliet**    That may be, sir, when I may be a wife.

20 **Paris**    That may be, must be, love, on Thursday next.

**Juliet**    What must be, shall be.

# Act four

## Scene 1

*Friar Lawrence's cell. Enter* **Friar Lawrence** *and* **Paris**

**Friar Lawrence**   On Thursday, sir? That's very soon.

**Paris**   My father-in-law Capulet wants it that way. I'm not
inclined to slow him down.

**Friar Lawrence**   You say you don't know the lady's attitude?
This is very irregular. I don't like it.

**Paris**   She is crying excessively over Tybalt's death, so
therefore I've talked very little about love. Love and tears do
not live well together. Her father considers it is dangerous for
grief to dominate her, and in his wisdom, hastens our
marriage to stop her tears. She broods too much on her own,
and company might cure her. Now you know the reason for
the haste.

**Friar Lawrence**   [*to himself*] Would that I didn't know why it
should be postponed! [*To* **Paris**] Look, sir, here comes the lady
towards my cell.

[*Enter* **Juliet**]

**Paris**   A happy coincidence. My lady and my wife.

**Juliet**   That may be sir, when I may be a wife.

**Paris**   That 'may be' *must* be, my love, on Thursday next.

**Juliet**   'What must be, shall be'.

**Friar Lawrence**                    That's a certain text.

**Paris**   Come you to make confession to this father?

**Juliet**   To answer that, I should confess to you.

**Paris**   Do not deny to him that you love me.

25 **Juliet**   I will confess to you that I love him.

**Paris**   So will ye, I am sure, that you love me.

**Juliet**   If I do so, it will be of more price
Being spoke behind your back than to your face.

**Paris**   Poor soul, thy face is much abused with tears.

30 **Juliet**   The tears have got small victory by that,
For it was bad enough before their spite.

**Paris**   Thou wrong'st it more than tears with that report.

**Juliet**   That is no slander, sir, which is a truth,
And what I spake, I spake it to my face.

35 **Paris**   Thy face is mine, and thou hast slandered it.

**Juliet**   It may be so, for it is not mine own.
Are you at leisure, holy father, now,
Or shall I come to you at evening mass?

**Friar Lawrence**   My leisure serves me, pensive daughter,
40    now.
My lord, we must entreat the time alone.

**Paris**   God shield I should disturb devotion.
Juliet, on Thursday early will I rouse ye.
Till then, adieu and keep this holy kiss.

[*Exit*]

**Friar Lawrence**    That's a true saying.

**Paris**    Have you come to make confession to this Father?

**Juliet**    If I answered that, I'd be confessing to you.

**Paris**    Don't deny to him that you love me.

**Juliet**    I will confess to you that I love him.

**Paris**    You'll also confess, I'm sure, that you love me?

**Juliet**    If I did, it would be worth more being spoken behind your back than if I said it to your face.

**Paris**    Poor soul, your face is blotched with crying.

**Juliet**    Small victory to my tears. It was bad enough before.

**Paris**    You do yourself more wrong in saying that, than did your tears.

**Juliet**    There's no slander, sir, in telling the truth. What I said, I said to my face.

**Paris**    Your face is mine: and you have slandered it.

**Juliet**    That may be so. It is no longer my own. [*Breaking the exchange*] Are you free now, Father, or shall I come to you at evening Mass?

**Friar Lawrence**    It would be convenient for me now, my sorrowing daughter. [*To* **Paris**] My lord, I must ask you to leave us.

**Paris**    God forbid that I should interrupt religious rites. Juliet, I'll wake you early on Thursday. Till then, adieu, and accept this holy kiss.

[*He kisses her modestly and leaves*]

45 **Juliet**   O shut the door, and when thou hast done so,
    Come weep with me, past hope, past cure, past help!

**Friar Lawrence**   O Juliet, I already know thy grief;
    It strains me past the compass of my wits.
    I hear thou must – and nothing may prorogue it –
50     On Thursday next be married to this County.

**Juliet**   Tell me not, Friar, that thou hearest of this,
    Unless thou tell me how I may prevent it.
    If in thy wisdom thou canst give no help,
    Do thou but call my resolution wise,
55     And with this knife I'll help it presently.
    God joined my heart and Romeo's, thou our hands;
    And ere this hand, by thee to Romeo's sealed,
    Shall be the label to another deed,
    Or my true heart with treacherous revolt
60     Turn to another, this shall slay them both.
    Therefore, out of thy long-experienced time
    Give me some present counsel, or behold:
    'Twixt my extremes and me this bloody knife
    Shall play the umpire, arbitrating that
65     Which the commission of thy years and art
    Could to no issue of true honour bring.
    Be not so long to speak. I long to die
    If what thou speak'st speak not of remedy.

**Friar Lawrence**   Hold, daughter. I do spy a kind of hope
70     Which craves as desperate an execution
    As that is desperate which we would prevent.
    If, rather than to marry County Paris,
    Thou hast the strength of will to slay thyself,
    Then is it likely thou wilt undertake
75     A thing like death to chide away this shame,
    That cop'st with death himself to scape from it.
    And if thou dar'st, I'll give thee remedy.

**Juliet**    [*to the Friar*] Oh, shut the door! And when you've done that, come and weep with me – past hope, past care, past help!

**Friar Lawrence**    Oh Juliet, I already know your grief. It is beyond all bearing for me. I hear that you must be married to the Count on Thursday next – and nothing can postpone it.

**Juliet**    Don't tell me, Friar, that you've heard of this, unless you also tell me how I can stop it. If, in spite of your wisdom, you can offer no help, just say my intention is sensible and I'll implement it straight away with this knife. [*She draws one from her robe*] God joined my heart and Romeo's: you joined our hands. And before this hand (sealed to Romeo's by you) shall seal a second marriage contract, or my faithful heart treacherously defect to someone else, this [*she gestures with her knife*] shall slay them both. Therefore, from your long years of experience, give me some advice. Otherwise, take note! This lethal knife will arbitrate between my desperate situation and myself. It will make the decision that neither the wisdom of your age, nor your professional skill, could honourably resolve. Answer me quickly. I long to die, if your reply provides no remedy.

**Friar Lawrence**    [*his hand on the knife*] Hold, daughter! I can see a sort of hope. It demands as dangerous a course of action as the matter is dangerous that we want to prevent. If you've got the strength of will to kill yourself rather than marry Count Paris, then you'll probably undergo a state resembling death to avert this shame. You've already contemplated actual death on that account. If you have the nerve, I have the remedy.

**Juliet**    O, bid me leap, rather than marry Paris,
80    From off the battlements of any tower,
Or walk in thievish ways, or bid me lurk
Where serpents are. Chain me with roaring bears,
Or hide me nightly in a charnel-house
O'ercovered quite with dead men's rattling bones,
With reeky shanks and yellow chapless skulls.
85    Or bid me go into a new-made grave,
And hide me with a dead man in his shroud –
Things that, to hear them told, have made me tremble –
And I will do it without fear or doubt.
To live an unstained wife to my sweet love.

90    **Friar Lawrence**    Hold then. Go home, be merry, give consent
To marry Paris. Wednesday is tomorrow;
Tomorrow night look that thou lie alone.
Let not the Nurse lie with thee in thy chamber.
Take thou this vial, being then in bed,
95    And this distilling liquor drink thou off;
When presently through all thy veins shall run
A cold and drowsy humour, for no pulse
Shall keep his native progress, but surcease;
No warmth, no breath shall testify thou livest,
100    The roses in thy lips and cheeks shall fade
To wanny ashes, thy eyes' windows fall
Like death when he shuts up the day of life.
Each part deprived of supple government
Shall stiff and stark and cold appear, like death,
105    And in this borrowed likeness of shrunk death
Thou shall continue two and forty hours
And then awake as from a pleasant sleep.
Now when the bridegroom in the morning comes
To rouse thee from thy bed, there art thou, dead.
110    Then as the manner of our country is,
In thy best robes, uncovered on the bier

**Juliet**    Rather than marry Paris, ask me to leap from the
battlements of any tower, or walk where there are thieves, or
loiter where snakes are. Chain me with roaring bears; hide me
nightly in a mortuary, covered over completely with dead
men's rattling bones, stinking limbs, and yellow jawless
skulls. Order me to enter a new-made grave, to hide with a
dead man in his shroud – things that have made me tremble
just to talk about – and I'll do it without fear or doubt, to live a
faithful wife to my sweet love.

**Friar Lawrence**    Right, then. Go home, be cheerful, and say
you'll marry Paris. Tomorrow is Wednesday. Tomorrow night
make sure you sleep alone. Don't let the Nurse sleep with you
in your room. When you're in bed, take this small bottle and
swallow this distilled liquid. Soon, a feeling will run through
your veins of cold and drowsiness. Your pulse will cease. No
warmth, no breath, will indicate that you're alive. The redness
of your lips and cheeks will fade to a pale ashen colour. Your
eyelids will close as if death had signalled your life's end. Each
part of you, losing its movement, will appear stiff, and stark,
and cold, like death. And in this death-like coma you'll remain
for forty-two hours, and then awake as if from a pleasant
sleep. When the bridegroom comes in the morning to get you
up, there you are, dead. Then, as is the custom in our country,
you'll be carried on an open bier in your best clothes to the

Thou shall be borne to that same ancient vault
Where all the kindred of the Capulets lie.
In the meantime, against thou shalt awake,
115 Shall Romeo by my letters know our drift
And hither shall he come, and he and I
Will watch thy waking, and that very night
Shall Romeo bear thee hence to Mantua,
And this shall free thee from this present shame,
120 If no inconstant toy nor womanish fear
Abate thy valour in the acting it.

**Juliet**   Give me, give me! O tell not me of fear.

**Friar Lawrence**   Hold. Get you gone. Be strong and
prosperous
125 In this resolve. I'll send a friar with speed
To Mantua with my letters to thy lord.

**Juliet**   Love give me strength, and strength shall help afford.
Farewell, dear father.

[*Exeunt*]


## Scene 2

*Capulet's house. Enter* **Capulet**, **Lady Capulet**, **Nurse** *and two or
three* **Servants**


**Capulet**   So many guests invite as here are writ.

[*Exit* **Servant**]

Sirrah, go hire me twenty cunning cooks.

ancient tomb where all the kinfolk of the Capulets lie. In the meantime, in readiness for your awakening, Romeo will know of our plan from my letters, and he'll come here. He and I will be there when you wake, and that same night Romeo will carry you off to Mantua. This will free you from this shameful predicament, provided neither irresolution nor some womanish fear steals your courage as you are doing it.

**Juliet**    Give it me! Give it me! Don't talk to me of fear!

**Friar Lawrence**    Here then. [*He hands her the bottle*] Off you go. Be firm and successful in your determination. I'll send a friar immediately to Mantua, with letters to your husband.

**Juliet**    Love give me strength! Strength is what I need. Farewell, dear Father.

[*They go*]


# Scene 2

*Capulet's house. Enter* **Capulet, Lady Capulet, Nurse** *and* **Servants**


**Capulet**    [*handing a paper to a* **Servant**] Invite the guests on this list. [*The* **Servant** *goes. To another*] You, fellow: go and hire me twenty first-class cooks.

**Servant**   You shall have none ill, sir, for I'll try if they can lick
    their fingers.

5 **Capulet**   How canst thou try them so?

**Servant**   Marry sir, 'tis an ill cook that cannot lick his own
    fingers; therefore he that cannot lick his fingers goes not with
    me.

**Capulet**   Go, be gone.

[*Exit* **Servant**]

10   We shall be much unfurnished for this time.
    What, is my daughter gone to Friar Lawrence?

**Nurse**   Ay, forsooth.

**Capulet**   Well, he may chance to do some good on her.
    A peevish self-willed harlotry it is.

[*Enter* **Juliet**]

15 **Nurse**   See where she comes from shrift with merry look.

**Capulet**   How now, my headstrong: where have you
    been gadding?

**Juliet**   Where I have learnt me to repent the sin
    Of disobedient opposition
20   To you and your behests, and am enjoined
    By holy Lawrence to fall prostrate here,
    To beg your pardon. Pardon, I beseech you.
    Henceforward I am ever ruled by you.

**Capulet**   Send for the County, go tell him of this.
25   I'll have this knot knit up tomorrow morning.

**Juliet**   I met the youthful lord at Lawrence' cell,

**Servant**   You'll have no bad ones, sir, because I'll test whether they can lick their fingers.

**Capulet**   Eh? What sort of test is that?

**Servant**   Well, sir, it's a poor cook who won't lick his own fingers. So anyone who won't, doesn't get the job!

**Capulet**   [*laughing*] Be off with you! [*The* **Servant** *goes*] We're not prepared for this great day. Has my daughter gone to Friar Lawrence?

**Nurse**   Yes, indeed.

**Capulet**   Well, maybe he'll do some good with her. A peevish, obstinate, good-for-nothing she is!

[*Enter* **Juliet**]

**Nurse**   Look how happy she's come back from confession!

**Capulet**   Well, now, my stubborn one. Where have you been traipsing?

**Juliet**   Where I've learned to repent my sin of disobedience and opposition to you and your commands. The holy Father Lawrence counsels me to fall at your feet and beg your pardon. [*She kneels*] Pardon, I beg you. In future, I'll always be obedient.

**Capulet**   Send for Count Paris! Tell him this! I'll have the marriage ceremony tomorrow morning!

**Juliet**   I met the young lord at Lawrence's cell, and showed him

And gave him what becomed love I might,
Not stepping o'er the bounds of modesty.

**Capulet**    Why, I am glad on't. This is well. Stand
30      up.
This is as't should be. Let me see the County.
Ay marry. Go, I say, and fetch him hither.
Now afore God, this reverend Holy Friar,
All our whole city is much bound to him.

35 **Juliet**    Nurse, will you go with me into my closet,
To help me sort such needful ornaments
As you think fit to furnish me tomorrow?

**Lady Capulet**    No, not till Thursday, there is time enough.

40 **Capulet**    Go, Nurse, go with her. We'll to church
tomorrow.

[*Exeunt* **Juliet** *and* **Nurse**]

**Lady Capulet**    We shall be short in our provision,
'Tis now near night.

**Capulet**                    'Tush I will stir about,
And all things shall be well, I warrant thee, wife.
45 Go thou to Juliet, help to deck up her.
I'll not to bed tonight, let me alone.
I'll play the housewife for this once. What ho!
They are all forth. Well, I will walk myself
To County Paris, to prepare up him
50 Against tomorrow. My heart is wondrous light
Since this same wayward girl is so reclaimed.

[*Exeunt*]

such affection as was befitting without immodesty.

**Capulet**   Well, I'm very pleased. This is splendid. Stand up! [*He helps her to rise*] This is as it should be. I must see the Count. Yes indeed. [*to servant*] Go, I say, and fetch him here. [*A* **Servant** *leaves*] Now before God: this reverend holy Friar – the whole of our city is indebted to him!

**Juliet**   Nurse, will you go with me to my room and help me sort out the things you think I'll need tomorrow?

**Lady Capulet**   No – not till Thursday. That's time enough.

**Capulet**   Go, Nurse; go with her. We'll go to church tomorrow.

[**Juliet** *and the* **Nurse** *go*]


**Lady Capulet**   We'll be short of food. It's nearly night-time!

**Capulet**   Tush! I'll get things moving, all will be well, I assure you wife. Go to Juliet. Help to deck her up. No bed for me tonight. Leave it to me. I'll be the housewife for this once. [*He calls a servant*] Hey, there! They've all gone out. Well, I'll walk to Count Paris myself, to get him prepared for tomorrow. I feel so happy, now this wilful girl of mine's reformed!

[*They go*]

## Scene 3

*Juliet's bedroom. Enter* **Juliet** *and* **Nurse**

**Juliet**    Ay, those attires are best. But, gentle Nurse,
I pray thee leave me to myself tonight,
For I have need of many orisons
To move the heavens to smile upon my state,
5    Which, well thou know'st, is cross and full of sin.

[*Enter* **Lady Capulet**]

**Lady Capulet**    What, are you busy, ho? Need you my help?

**Juliet**    No madam. We have culled such necessaries
As are behoveful for our state tomorrow.
So please you, let me now be left alone
10    And let the Nurse this night sit up with you,
For I am sure you have your hands full all
In this so sudden business.

**Lady Capulet**                        Good night.
Get thee to bed and rest, for thou hast need.

[*Exeunt* **Lady Capulet** *and* **Nurse**]

**Juliet**    Farewell. God knows when we shall meet again.
15    I have a faint cold fear thrills through my veins,
That almost freezes up the heat of life.
I'll call them back again to comfort me.
Nurse! What should she do here?
My dismal scene I needs must act alone.
20    Come vial.
What if this mixture do not work at all?
Shall I be married then tomorrow morning?

## Scene 3

*Juliet's bedroom. Enter* **Juliet** *and the* **Nurse**

**Juliet**   Yes, those clothes are best. Gentle Nurse, please leave me to myself tonight. I've need of many prayers to persuade God to smile on me. You well know I'm stubborn and full of sin.

[*Enter* **Lady Capulet**]

**Lady Capulet**   What, are you busy there? Do you need my help?

**Juliet**   No, madam, we've chosen the right sort of things for tomorrow's occasion. So if you please, let me be left alone now, and let the Nurse sit up with you tonight. I'm sure you all have your hands full, with this happening so suddenly.

**Lady Capulet**   Good night. Go to bed and rest. You need it.

[**Lady Capulet** *and the* **Nurse** *leave*]

**Juliet**   Farewell. God knows when we shall meet again. A chill of fear runs through my veins that almost freezes me to death. I'll call them back again to comfort me! [*She calls*] Nurse! [*Pause: there is no answer*] What could she do? This is a grim scene that I've got to act alone. [*She takes up Friar Lawrence's small bottle*] Come then, vial! [*She pauses*] What if this mixture doesn't work at all? Shall I be married then, tomorrow

No, no. This shall forbid it.    [*She lays down her knife*]

Lie thou there.

What if it be a poison which the Friar
25  Subtly hath ministered to have me dead,
Lest in this marriage he should be dishonoured
Because he married me before to Romeo?
I fear it is; and yet methinks it should not,
30  For he hath still been tried a holy man.
How if, when I am laid into the tomb,
I wake before the time that Romeo
Come to redeem me? There's a fearful point!
Shall I not then be stifled in the vault,
35  To whose foul mouth no healthsome air breathes in,
And there die strangled ere my Romeo comes?
O, if I live, is it not very like
The horrible conceit of death and night,
Together with the terror of the place –
40  As in a vault, an ancient receptacle,
Where, for this many hundred years, the bones
Of all my buried ancestors are packed;
Where bloody Tybalt yet but green in earth.
Lies festering in his shroud; where, as they say,
45  At some hours in the night spirits resort –
Alack, alack! Is it not like that I,
So early waking, what with loathsome smells
And shrieks like mandrakes torn out of the earth,
That living mortals, hearing them run mad –
50  O, if I wake shall I not be distraught,
Environed with all these hideous fears,
And madly play with my forefathers' joints,
And pluck the mangled Tybalt from his shroud.
And in this rage, with some great kinsman's bone,
As with a club, dash out my desperate brains?
55  O look! Methinks I see my cousin's ghost,
Seeking out Romeo that did spit his body

morning? No, no! [*She takes out a knife*] This will prevent it.
You lie there! [*She puts it beside the bed*] What if it's a poison
that the Friar has cunningly provided, to kill me in case this
marriage brings disgrace upon him, because he married me to
Romeo before? I fear it is! And then again, I don't think so, he's
always proved a pious man. What if I wake before Romeo
comes to rescue me, when I'm laid out in the tomb? That's a
frightening thought! Won't I then be suffocated in the vault,
which never gets fresh air, and die there strangled before my
Romeo comes? Or, if I live, won't eerie thoughts about death
and night-time, together with the terror of the place . . . it being
a tomb, an ancient sepulchre, where for many hundred years
past, the bones of all my buried ancestors are stored, there
Tybalt lies newly buried, bloody, and rotting in his shroud, and
there, so they say, ghosts resort at certain times of night . . .
Alas, alas! Isn't it likely that wakening early – what with
loathsome smells, and shrieks like those that mandrakes
make when torn from the ground, turning human beings mad!
Oh, if I wake – won't I go out of my mind, closeted with all
those hideous terrors, and play insanely with my ancestors'
skeletons? And pull the mangled Tybalt from his shroud? And
in my madness dash my desperate brains out, using some
great relative's bone as a club? Oh, look! I think I see my
cousin's ghost, looking for Romeo, who spitted his body on

Upon a rapier's point. Stay, Tybalt, stay!
Romeo, I come! This do I drink to thee.

[*She falls on her bed*]

## Scene 4

*The hall in Capulet's house. Enter* **Lady Capulet** *and* **Nurse**

**Lady Capulet**    Hold, take these keys and fetch more spices,
Nurse.

**Nurse**    They call for dates and quinces in the pastry.

[*Enter* **Capulet**]

**Capulet**    Come, stir, stir, stir! The second cock hath crowed,
5    The curfew bell hath rung, 'tis three o'clock.
Look to the baked meats, good Angelica;
Spare not for cost.

**Nurse**                    Go, ye cot-quean, go.
Get you to bed. Faith, you'll be sick tomorrow
For this night's watching.

10 **Capulet**    No, not a whit. What! I have watched ere now
All night for lesser cause and ne'er been sick.

**Lady Capulet**    Ay, you have been a mouse-hunt in your time.
But I will watch you from such watching now.

[*Exeunt* **Lady Capulet** *and* **Nurse**]

**Capulet**    A jealous hood, a jealous hood!

the end of a rapier. Stop, Tybalt! Stop! Romeo, I come! I drink this for you!

[*She falls on her bed*]

## Scene 4

*The hall of Capulet's house. Enter* **Lady Capulet** *and the* **Nurse**, *who is carrying a basket of herbs*

**Lady Capulet**    Stop. Take these keys and fetch more spices, Nurse.

**Nurse**    They want more dates and quinces in the pastryroom.

[**Capulet** *enters*]

**Capulet**    Come on – hurry up! hurry up! It's three in the morning: the cock has crowed and the curfew bell has rung. [*to the* **Nurse**] See there's plenty of cooked meat, Angelica – don't spare the cost!

**Nurse**    Begone, you house-husband you! Get to bed! Sure, you'll be sick tomorrow from lack of sleep!

**Capulet**    No, not a bit. What? I've stayed up all night for lesser reasons and never been sick.

**Lady Capulet**    Yes, you've been after women in your time! But I'll keep an eye on you now! [**Lady Capulet** *and* **Nurse** *leave*]

**Capulet**:    She's a jealous one! a jealous one!

[*Enter three or four* **Servants** *with spits and logs and baskets*]

15                                    Now fellow, what is there?

**First Servant**    Things for the cook, sir, but I know not what.

**Capulet**    Make haste, make haste!

[*Exit* **First Servant**]

Sirrah, fetch drier logs!
Call Peter, he will show thee where they are.

**Second Servant**    I have a head, sir, that will find out logs
20      And never trouble Peter for the matter.

**Capulet**    Mass and well said! A merry whoreson, ha!
Thou shalt be loggerhead!

[*Exit* **Second Servant**]

Good faith! 'Tis day!
The County will be here with music straight,
For so he said he would. I hear him near.
25      Nurse! Wife! What ho! What, Nurse, I say!

[*Enter* **Nurse**]

Go waken Juliet, go, and trim her up.
I'll go and chat with Paris. Hie, make haste,
Make haste! The bridegroom he is come already.
Make haste I say.

[*Exeunt*]

[**Servants** *enter with meat-spits, logs, and baskets*]

Now what's there, eh?

**Servant**    Things for the cook, sir, but I don't know what.

**Capulet**    Hurry, hurry, man. Fetch drier logs, Call Peter. He'll
show you where they are.

**Servant**    I'm good at finding logs. No need to bother Peter.

**Capulet**    Great – well said! You're a witty rascal! [*He laughs*]
We'll call you 'blockhead'. [*the* **Servant** *goes*] Good gracious –
it's day! The County will be here with the musicians any
moment. He said he would. [*The sound of music is heard*] I can
hear him approaching. Nurse! Wife! Hey there! What, Nurse, I
say!

[*the* **Nurse** *enters*]

Go and awaken Juliet. Go and fancy her up. I'll go and chat with
Paris. Quick – make haste! Make haste! The bridegroom's
already here. Make haste, I say!

[*They all leave*]

## Scene 5

*Juliet's bedroom. Enter* **Nurse**


**Nurse**    Mistress! What. mistress! Juliet! Fast, I warrant her,
    she.
    Why, lamb. why, lady, fie! You slug-abed!
    Why, love, I say! Madam! Sweetheart! Why, bride!
5    What, not a word? You take your pennyworths now.
    Sleep for a week; for the next night, I warrant,
    The County Paris hath set up his rest
    That you shall rest but little! God forgive me!
    Marry and amen. How sound is she asleep!
10    I needs must wake her. Madam, madam, madam!
    Ay, let the County take you in your bed,
    He'll fright you up, i'faith. Will it not be?
    What, dressed, and in your clothes, and down again?
    I must needs wake you. Lady! Lady! Lady!
15    Alas, alas! Help, help! My lady's dead!
    O well-a-day that ever I was born.
    Some aqua vitae, ho! My lord! My lady!

[*Enter* **Lady Capulet**]


**Lady Capulet**    What noise is here?

**Nurse**                     O lamentable day!

20 **Lady Capulet**    What is the matter?

**Nurse**                  Look, look! O heavy day!

**Lady Capulet**    O me, O me! My child, my only life.
    Revive, look up, or I will die with thee.
    Help, help! Call help!

[*Enter* **Capulet**]

## Scene 5

*Juliet's bedroom. The bed-curtains are closed*

**Nurse**    Mistress! Mistress! Juliet! Fast asleep, I'll be bound, she
is. My lamb! My lady! Tut! You lazybones! Why, love I say!
Madam! Sweetheart! Bride! What, not a word? Take you
penn'orth of sleep now: sleep for a week! Tomorrow night
Count Paris won't give you any rest: he'll be up all night. I'll
bet! [*She apologizes for her bawdy jest*] May God forgive me!
[*She crosses herself*] Amen, to be sure! How sound asleep she
is! I'll have to wake her. Madam! Madam! Madam! Oh yes, let
the Count catch you in your bed – he'll have you up, indeed!
Won't you wake? [*She opens the bed curtains*] What, dressed
in your clothes and back in bed again? I'll have to wake you up.
Lady, lady, lady! [*She suddenly realizes* **Juliet** *is not sleeping
naturally*] Alas! Alas! Help! Help! My lady's dead! Oh, rue the
day that I was ever born! Some brandy, there! My lord! My
lady!

[*Enter* **Lady Capulet**]

**Lady Capulet**    What's all this noise?

**Nurse**    Oh sorrowful day!

**Lady Capulet**    What's the matter?

**Nurse**    Look, look! Oh, tragic day!

**Lady Capulet**    Oh no! Oh no! My child, my only one; wake up;
look up, or I'll die with you! Help! Help! Call for help!

[*Enter* **Capulet**]

**Capulet**    For shame, bring Juliet forth, her lord is come.

**Nurse**    She's dead, deceased! She's dead! Alack the day!

25 **Lady Capulet**    Alack the day! She's dead, she's dead, she's
dead!

**Capulet**    Ha! Let me see her. Out alas. She's cold,
Her blood is settled and her joints are stiff.
Life and these lips have long been separated.
30 Death lies on her like an untimely frost
Upon the sweetest flower of all the field.

**Nurse**    O lamentable day!

**Lady Capulet**                    O woeful time!

**Capulet**    Death, that hath ta'en her hence to make me wail
Ties up my tongue and will not let me speak.

[*Enter* **Friar Lawrence** *and* **Paris** *and* **Musicians**]

35 **Friar Lawrence**    Come, is the bride ready to go to church?

**Capulet**    Ready to go, but never to return.
O son, the night before thy wedding day
Hath Death lain with thy wife. There she lies,
Flower as she was, deflowered by him.
40 Death is my son-in-law, Death is my heir.
My daughter he hath wedded. I will die,
And leave him all: life, living, all is Death's.

**Paris**    Have I thought long to see this morning's face,
And doth it give me such a sight as this?

45 **Lady Capulet**    Accursed, unhappy, wretched, hateful day.
Most miserable hour that e'er time saw
In lasting labour of his pilgrimage.
But one, poor one, one poor and loving child,

**Capulet**   Shame on you. Bring Juliet: her bridegroom has arrived.

**Nurse**   She's dead! Dead and gone! She's dead, dead, alas the day!

**Capulet**   What? Let me see her! [*He groans*] Oh! She's cold. Her blood has set; her limbs are stiff. Life has long since passed from her lips. The frost of an untimely death lies upon her: upon the sweetest flower of all the field.

**Nurse**   Oh day of sorrow!

**Capulet**   Death, who took her to make me howl, ties my tongue and stops my speech.

[*Enter* **Friar Lawrence, Paris** *and* **Musicians**]

**Friar Lawrence**   Come: is the bride ready for church?

**Capulet**   Ready to go – but she'll never return. [*To* **Paris**] Oh, son; on the eve of your wedding day Death has slept with your wife. There she lies: a flower in life, deflowered by him. Death is my son-in-law. Death is my heir. He has married my daughter. I will die and leave him everything. Life, living, all belongs to Death!

**Paris**   Have I looked forward to this morning, only to see a sight like this?

**Lady Capulet**   Cursed, unhappy, wretched, hateful day! The most miserable hour that Time has ever known! An only child, one poor and loving child, my only source of pleasure and

But one thing to rejoice and solace in,
50  And cruel Death hath catched it from my sight.

**Nurse**    O woe! O woeful, woeful, woeful day.
Most lamentable day! Most woeful day
That ever, ever I did yet behold.
O day, O day, O day, O hateful day.
55  Never was seen so black a day as this.
O woeful day, O woeful day.

**Paris**    Beguiled, divorced, wronged, spited, slain,
Most detestable Death, by thee beguiled,
By cruel, cruel, thee, quite overthrown.
60  O love, O life, not life, but love in death.

**Capulet**    Despised, distressed, hated, martyred, killed.
Uncomfortable time, why cam'st thou now
To murder, murder our solemnity?
O child, O child! My soul and not my child,
65  Dead art thou. Alack, my child is dead,
And with my child my joys are buried.

**Friar Lawrence**    Peace, ho, for shame. Confusion's cure lives
    not
In these confusions. Heaven and yourself
70  Had part in this fair maid, now heaven hath all,
And all the better is it for the maid.
Your part in her you could not keep from death,
But heaven keeps his part in eternal life.
The most you sought was her promotion,
75  For 'twas your heaven she should be advanced,
And weep ye now, seeing she is advanced
Above the clouds, as high as heaven itself?
O, in this love you love your child so ill
That you run mad, seeing that she is well.
80  She's not well married that lives married long,
But she's best married that dies married young.

delight – and cruel Death has snatched her from me!

**Nurse**   Oh misery! Oh wretched, wretched, wretched day! The most sorrowful day, the most wretched day, that I've ever, ever known! What a day, a day, a day! What a hateful day! There was never a day as black as this! Oh, wretched day! Oh, wretched day!

**Paris**   Deceived, divorced, wronged, spited, murdered! Deceived by Death at its most hateful! Quite overcome by Death in all its cruelty! Oh, love! Oh, life! Not living, but still my love in death!

**Capulet**   Despised, distressed, hated, martyred, killed! Merciless time – why choose now to murder, to murder our festivities? Oh, child! Oh, child! My soul – not my child! You are dead! Alas, my child is dead, and happiness is buried with my child!

**Friar Lawrence**   Quiet, everyone, for shame! Calamity is not cured by weeping and wailing. Heaven and yourselves had shares in this lovely girl: now Heaven has all of her, and it's all to her advantage. You could not save her mortal body from Death: heaven has her soul eternally. Your ambition was to see her well set-up; your ideal for her was a good marriage: do you mourn now, knowing she is elevated above the clouds – as high as heaven itself? This sort of love means that you love her so little that you're demented at the thought that she's so fortunate. Lengthy marriage doesn't mean happy marriage. Those are best married who die in the early days.

Dry up your tears, and stick your rosemary
On this fair corse, and, as the custom is,
All in her best array bear her to church.
85  For though fond nature bids us all lament,
Yet nature's tears are reason's merriment.

**Capulet**    All things that we ordained festival
Turn from their office to black funeral:
Our instruments to melancholy bells,
90  Our wedding cheer to sad burial feast,
Our solemn hymns to sullen dirges change,
Our bridal flowers serve for a buried corse,
And all things change them to the contrary.

**Friar Lawrence**    Sir, go you in, and madam, go with him,
95  And go, Sir Paris. Everyone prepare
To follow this fair corse unto her grave.
The heavens do lour upon you for some ill;
Move them no more by crossing their high will.

[*Exeunt all but the* **Nurse** *and* **Musicians**, *casting rosemary on*
**Juliet** *and shutting the curtains*]

**First Musician**    Faith, we may put up our pipes and be gone.

100  **Nurse**    Honest good fellows, ah put up, put up,
For well you know this is a pitiful case.

**First Musician**    Ay, by my troth, the case may be amended.

[*Exit* **Nurse**]

[*Enter* **Peter**]

**Peter**    Musicians, O musicians, 'Heart's ease', Heart's ease'!
O, and you will have me live, play 'Heart's ease'.

105  **First Musician**    Why 'Heart's ease'?

Dry your tears. Put funeral flowers on her beautiful corpse, in the customary manner. In her finest clothes carry her to church. Emotion makes it natural to cry – reason mocks our tears of sorrow.

**Capulet**  Everything we ordered for the festival must now be turned to black for the funeral: our music, to melancholy bells, our wedding banquet, to a sad burial feast, our marriage hymns to mournful dirges; our bridal flowers, to wreaths. Change everything to the opposite.

**Friar Lawrence**  Sir, go now. And madam, go with him. And go, Sir Paris. Let everyone prepare to follow this lovely corpse to her grave. The heavens frown upon you for some wrong you've done: don't anger them further by antagonizing them.

[*Rosemary is placed on* **Juliet**'s *body as a token of remembrance. The curtains are closed. Everyone leaves but the* **Nurse** *and the* **Musicians**]

**First Musician**  Well, we must pack up our instruments and be gone. [*He turns to his delapidated equipment*]

**Nurse**  Dear good fellows, yes, pack up, pack up. You well know this is a case for sorrow.

**First Musician**  Yes, indeed. [*Showing her a broken instrument case*] This one needs mending.

[*The* **Nurse** *leaves and* **Peter** *enters*]

**Peter**  Musicians, oh musicians! Play me 'Heart's Ease'! 'Heart's Ease'! If you want to keep me going, play 'Heart's Ease'.

**First Musician**  Why 'Heart's Ease'?

**Peter**    O musicians, because my heart itself plays 'My heart is full'. O play me some merry dump to comfort me.

**First Musician**    Not a dump we! 'Tis no time to play now.

**Peter**    You will not then?

110 **First Musician**    No.

**Peter**    I will then give it you soundly.

**First Musician**    What will you give us?

**Peter**    No money, on my faith, but the gleek! I will give you the minstrel.

115 **First Musician**    Then will I give you the serving-creature.

**Peter**    Then will I lay the serving-creature's dagger on your pate. I will carry no crotchets. I'll re you, I'll fa you. Do you note me?

**First Musician**    And you re us and fa us, you note us.

120 **Second Musician**    Pray you put up your dagger and put out your wit.

**Peter**    Then have at you with my wit. I will dry-beat you with an iron wit, and put up my iron dagger. Answer me like men.

'When griping griefs the heart doth wound,
125        And doleful dumps the mind oppress,
        Then music with her silver sound' –

Why 'silver sound'? Why 'music with her silver sound'?
What say you, Simon Catling?

**First Musician**    Marry, sir, because silver hath a sweet sound.

130 **Peter**    Pretty. What say you, Hugh Rebeck?

**Second Musician**    I say 'silver sound' because musicians sound for silver.

**Peter**   Oh, musicians – because my own heart is playing 'Heart Ache'. Oh, play me a cheerful dirge!

**First Musician**   Not a dirge, us. This is no time to be playing.

**Peter**   You won't, then?

**First Musician**   No.

**Peter**   Then I'll give you a beat.

**First Musician**   What'll you give us?

**Peter**   Not money, for sure! But a sign. [*He makes a rude one*] I'll call you a busker!

**First Musician**   Then I'll call you a skivvy!

**Peter**   In that case [*taking out his knife*] this skivvy's dagger will hit you on the head! I won't have you being crochety! [*He gets aggressive*] I'll 're' you! I'll 'fa' you! Do you note what I'm saying?

**First Musician**   'Re' and 'Fa' us, and you'll be taking note of us!

**Second Musician**   Please put your dagger away, and show your intelligence.

**Peter**   [*he makes a thrust with his weapon*] Have at you with my wit! I'll thrash you with a cutting remark, and then put my iron dagger away. [*He replaces it in its sheath*] Answer me like men. [*He recites*] –

> 'When griping grief does wound the heart
> And doleful dumps the mind oppress,
> Then music with her silver sound' –

Why 'silver sound'? Why 'music with her silver sound'? What do you think, Simon Catgut?

**First Musician**   Well, sir, because music has a sweet sound.

**Peter**   Clever! What do you think, Hugh Fiddle?

**Second Musician**   I say it's 'silver sound' because musicians play for money.

**Peter**  Pretty too. What say you, James Soundpost?

**Third Musician**  Faith, I know not what to say.

135 **Peter**  O, I cry you mercy, you are the singer. I will say for you. It is 'music with her silver sound' because musicians have no gold for sounding.

> 'Then music with her silver sound
> With speedy help doth lend redress.'

[*Exit*]

140 **First Musician**  What a pestilent knave is this same.

**Second Musician**  Hang him, Jack. Come, we'll in here, tarry for the mourners, and stay dinner.

[*Exeunt*]

**Peter**   Clever too! What do you say, James Soundingboard?

**Third Musician**   'Strewth, I don't know what to say.

**Peter**   Oh, I beg your pardon. You're the singer! I'll tell you. It's 'music with her silver sound' because musicians never get gold for playing:

> 'Then music with her silver sound
> With speedy help does lend redress'

[**Peter** *goes*]

**First Musician**   What an odious rogue he was!

**Second Musician**   To hell with him, Jack! Come on, we'll go in here, wait for the mourners and stay for dinner.

# Act five

## Scene 1

*A street in Mantua. Enter* **Romeo**


**Romeo**      If I may trust the flattering truth of sleep
My dreams presage some joyful news at hand.
My bosom's lord sits lightly in his throne
And all this day an unaccustomed spirit
5   Lifts me above the ground with cheerful thoughts.
I dreamt my lady came and found me dead –
Strange dream that gives a dead man leave to think! –
And breathed such life with kisses in my lips
That I revived and was an emperor.
10  Ah me, how sweet is love itself possessed
When but love's shadows are so rich in joy.

[*Enter* **Balthazar**, *Romeo's man*]

News from Verona! How, now Balthasar,
Dost thou not bring me letters from the Friar?
How doth my lady? Is my father well?
15  How doth my Juliet? That I ask again,
For nothing can be ill if she be well.

**Balthazar**    Then she is well and nothing can be ill.
Her body sleeps in Capels' monument,
And her immortal part with angels lives.
20  I saw her laid low in her kindred's vault
And presently took post to tell it you.
O pardon me for bringing these ill news,
Since you did leave it for my office, sir.

# Act five

## Scene 1

*A street in Mantua. Enter* **Romeo**

**Romeo**  If I can trust my pleasant dreams as truthful guides,
joyful news is on its way. My heart is ruled by love, and all day
long I've felt unusually cheerful. I dreamt my loved-one came
and found me dead – an odd dream, that let's a dead man
think! She gave me the kiss of life, and I revived, and was an
emperor! How sweet is genuine love, when love's fantasies
are so rich in happiness!

[*Enter* **Balthazar,** *Romeo's servant*]

News from Verona! Greetings, Balthazar. You've brought me
letters from the Friar? How is my wife? Is my father well? How
is my Juliet? I ask you that again, since nothing can be wrong if
she is well.

**Balthazar**  Then she is well, and nothing can be wrong. Her
body is asleep in the Capulet family tomb, and her soul is with
the angels. I saw her put to rest in the family vault, and came
post-haste to tell you of it. Pardon me for bringing this bad
news: it was a duty, sir, that you entrusted to me.

**Romeo**    Is it e'en so? Then I defy you, stars!
25    Thou know'st my lodging. Get me ink and paper,
And hire posthorses. I will hence tonight.

**Balthazar**    I do beseech you sir, have patience.
Your looks are pale and wild and do import
Some misadventure.

**Romeo**                        Tush, thou art deceived.
30    Leave me, and do the thing I bid thee do.
Hast thou no letters to me from the Friar?

**Balthazar**    No, my good lord.

**Romeo**                            No matter. Get thee gone.
And hire those horses. I'll be with thee straight.

[*Exit* **Balthazar**]

Well, Juliet, I will lie with thee tonight.
35    Let's see for means. O mischief thou art swift
To enter in the thoughts of desperate men.
I do remember an apothecary –
And hereabouts a dwells – which late I noted
In tattered weeds, with overwhelming brows,
40    Culling of simples. Meagre were his looks.
Sharp misery had worn him to the bones,
And in his needy shop a tortoise hung,
And alligator stuffed, and other skins
Of ill-shaped fishes; and about his shelves
45    A beggarly account of empty boxes,
Green earthen pots, bladders, and musty seeds,
Remnants of packthread, and old cakes of roses
Were thinly scattered to make up a show.
Noting this penury, to myself I said,
50    'And if a man did need a poison now,
Whose sale is present death in Mantua,

**Romeo**    Can it really be so? [*Shaking his fist at the sky*] Fate – I defy you! [*To* **Balthazar**] You know where I'm living: get me ink and paper, and hire posthorses. I'll set off tonight.

**Balthazar**    I beg you, sir, be brave. You look pale and distraught. Misfortune is indicated.

**Romeo**    Tush: you've got it wrong. Leave me, and do what I tell you. You have no letters from the Friar?

**Balthazar**    No, my good lord.

**Romeo**    It doesn't matter. Go now, and hire those horses. I'll join you soon.

[**Balthazar** *leaves*]

Well, Juliet, I shall lie with you tonight. Let's see how. How quickly desperate men harbour scheming thoughts! There's a chemist I remember who lives round here. I noticed him recently, dressed in tattered clothes, with bushy eyebrows, gathering herbs. He looked drawn – acute poverty had worn him down. In his shabby shop he had a tortoiseshell hanging, a stuffed alligator, and various skins of grotesque fishes. On his shelves, thinly scattered to make some sort of show, were a few empty boxes, green earthenware jars, old leather bottles and stale seeds, bits of string, and old rose-scented blocks. Noting this poverty, I said to myself 'If ever a man needed a poison, the sale of which is a capital offence in

Here lives a caitiff wretch would sell it him'.
O, this same thought did but forerun my need,
And this same needy man must sell it me.
55 As I remember, this should be the house.
Being holiday, the beggar's shop is shut.
What ho! Apothecary!

[*Enter* **Apothecary**]

**Apothecary**                    Who calls so loud?

**Romeo**    Come hither man. I see that thou art poor.
Hold, there is forty ducats. Let me have
60 A dram of poison, such soon-spreading gear
As will disperse itself through all the veins,
That the life-weary taker may fall dead,
And that the trunk may be discharged of breath
As violently as hasty powder fired
65 Doth hurry from the fatal cannon's womb.

**Apothecary**    Such mortal drugs I have, but Mantua's law
Is death to any he that utters them.

**Romeo**    Art thou so bare and full of wretchedness,
And fear'st to die? Famine is in thy cheeks,
70 Need and oppression starveth in thy eyes,
Contempt and beggary hangs upon thy back.
The world is not thy friend, nor the world's law;
The world affords no law to make thee rich;
Then be not poor, but break it, and take this.

75 **Apothecary**    My poverty, but not my will consents.

**Romeo**    I pay thy poverty and not thy will.

**Apothecary**    Put this in any liquid thing you will
And drink it off and if you had the strength
Of twenty men it would dispatch you straight.

Mantua, here lives a miserable wretch who'd sell it to him.'
Oh, that very thought anticipated my need and this selfsame
needy man must sell it me. As I remember it, this is his house:
being a holiday, the pauper's shop is closed. I say, there!
Chemist!

[*A* **Chemist** *enters*]

**Chemist**    Who shouts so loudly?

**Romeo**    Come here, man. I see you are poor. [**Romeo** *shows
him a bag of money*] Right. There's forty pounds. Let me have
a flask of poison, quick-acting stuff, that will spread itself
through every vein, and kill the suicide stone dead, taking his
breath away like gunpowder exploding inside a cannon.

**Chemist**    I have such lethal drugs, but it's death for anyone in
Mantua to offer them for sale.

**Romeo**    Can you be so threadbare and down on your luck, and
yet be afraid to die? Your cheeks are hollow; the hungry look
in your eyes shows need and distress. Utter poverty hangs on
your back. The world is no friend to you, nor the world's law:
the world gives you no chance to be rich. So don't be poor:
break the law, and take this. [*He thrusts his purse forward*]

**Chemist**    My poverty, not my conscience, accepts.

**Romeo**    It's your poverty I'm paying.

**Chemist**    [*giving* **Romeo** *a bottle*] Put this in any liquid you
choose, swallow it, and even if you had the strength of twenty
men, it would see you off immediately.

80 **Romeo**    There is thy gold – worse poison to men's souls,
Doing more murder in this loathsome world
Than these poor compounds that thou mayst not sell.
I sell thee poison, thou hast sold me none.
Farewell, buy food, and get thyself in flesh.
85 Come cordial, and not poison, go with me
To Juliet's grave, for there must I use thee.

[*Exeunt*]


## Scene 2

*Friar Lawrence's cell. Enter* **Friar John**


5 **Friar John**    Holy Franciscan Friar, Brother, ho!

[*Enter* **Friar Lawrence**]

**Friar Lawrence**    This same should be the voice of Friar John.
Welcome from Mantua. What says Romeo?
Or, if his mind be writ, give me his letter.

**Friar John**    Going to find a barefoot brother out,
One of our order, to associate me,
Here in this city visiting the sick,
And finding him, the searchers of the town,
Suspecting that we both were in a house
10 Where the infectious pestilence did reign,
Sealed up the doors and would not let us forth,
So that my speed to Mantua there was stayed.

**Friar Lawrence**    Who bare my letter then to Romeo?

**Romeo**   [*handing over the money*] Here is your gold – it's far
worse a poison to men's souls; it's the cause of far more
murder in this loathsome world then these wretched mixtures
you're forbidden to sell. I'm selling poison to you: you haven't
sold me any. Farewell! Buy some food, and put some flesh on
your bones!

[*The* **Chemist** *goes*]

[*Holding up the bottle*] Medicine and not poison, come with
me to Juliet's grave! I must use you there.

## Scene 2

*Friar Lawrence's cell. Enter* **Friar John**

**Friar John**   Holy Franciscan! Friar! Brother! Hello there!

[**Friar Lawrence** *comes from his inner room*]

**Friar Lawrence**   That sounds like Friar John's voice. Welcome
home from Mantua. What did Romeo say? Or, if his message
is written, let me have his letter.

**Friar John**   I went looking for a fellow-Franciscan to go with me.
He was visiting the sick. Having found him, the health officers,
suspecting we were in a house infected by the plague,
boarded up the doors, and wouldn't let us out. So I couldn't go
to Mantua.

**Friar Lawrence**   Who took the letter to Romeo, then?

**Friar John**   I could not send it – here it is again –
15  Nor get a messenger to bring it thee,
So fearful were they of infection.

**Friar Lawrence**   Unhappy fortune! By my brotherhood,
The letter was not nice but full of charge,
Of dear import, and the neglecting it
20  May do much danger. Friar John, go hence,
Get me an iron crow and bring it straight
Unto my cell.

**Friar John**              Brother I'll go and bring it thee.

[*Exit*]

**Friar Lawrence**   Now must I to the monument alone.
Within this three hours will fair Juliet wake.
25  She will beshrew me much that Romeo
Hath had no notice of these accidents,
But I will write again to Mantua,
And keep her at my cell till Romeo come.
Poor living corse, closed in a dead man's tomb.

[*Exit*]

## Scene 3

*The Capulet's vault. Enter* **Paris** *and his* **Page**

**Paris**   Give me the torch, boy. Hence and stand aloof.
Yet put it out, for I would not be seen.
Under yond yew trees lay thee all along,
Holding thy ear close to the hollow ground;

**Friar John**   I couldn't send it – here it is back again – nor get a messenger to deliver it to you. They were so afraid of infection.

**Friar Lawrence**   What dreadful luck! By my holy order, this wasn't a trivial letter, but one containing instructions of the most serious importance. Not to act on them could have very dangerous consequences. Friar John – go – get me an iron crowbar, and bring it to my cell immediately.

**Friar John**   Brother, I'll go and bring one to you.

[**Friar John** *leaves*]

**Friar Lawrence**   I must go to the tomb alone. Within the next three hours, fair Juliet will awake. She'll scold me greatly when she learns Romeo has had no warning of these developments. I'll write again to Mantua, and keep her at my cell till Romeo comes. Poor living corpse! Closeted in a dead man's tomb!

## Scene 3

*The Capulet vault. Enter* **Paris** *and his* **Page,** *carrying flowers*

**Paris**   Give me your torch, boy. Go, and keep at a distance. No – put it out: I don't want to be seen. Stretch out under the yew trees over there, and hold your ear close to the hollow ground.

5  So shall no foot upon the churchyard tread,
   Being loose, unfirm, with digging up of graves,
   But thou shalt hear it. Whistle then to me
   As signal that thou hear'st something approach.
   Give me those flowers. Do as I bid thee. Go.

10 **Page** I am almost afraid to stand alone
   Here in the churchyard. Yet I will adventure.

                 *[Retires]*

  [**Paris** *strews the tomb with flowers*]

  **Paris** Sweet flower, with flowers thy bridal bed I strew.
   O woe, thy canopy is dust and stones
   Which with sweet water nightly I will dew,
15  Or wanting that, with tears distilled by moans.
   The obsequies that I for thee will keep
   Nightly shall be to strew thy grave and weep.

  [**Page** *whistles*]

  The boy gives warning something doth approach.
   What cursed foot wanders this way tonight,
20  To cross my obsequies and true love's rite?
   What, with a torch? Muffle me, night, awhile.

  [**Paris** *retires*]

  [*Enter* **Romeo** *and* **Balthazar** *with a torch, a mattock and a crow of iron*]

  **Romeo** Give me that mattock and the wrenching iron.
   Hold, take this letter. Early in the morning
   See thou deliver it to my lord and father.

That way you'll hear any footstep in the churchyard, the ground being loose and unfirm with all the graves they've dug. If you hear anyone approach, whistle. Give me those flowers. Do as I tell you. Go!

[*The* **Page** *hands over the flowers*]

**Page**    [*to himself*] I'm almost afraid to be alone here in the churchyard, but I'll risk it.

[*He leaves*]

**Paris**    [*to* **Juliet** *who is lying on her funeral bier*] Sweet flower! I'll scatter flowers over your bridal bed. [*He does so*] Oh such sorrow! For a canopy you have dust and stones. I'll sprinkle them with perfumed water every night; or failing that, with tears produced by grieving. My mourning shall consist of strewing your grave with flowers each night, and weeping.

[*The* **Page** *whistles a warning*]

The boy is warning me. Someone's coming. Whose accursed foot comes this way tonight, interrupting my lamentations, and the rites of true love? And carrying a torch? Night must conceal me for a while.

[*He hides in the churchyard*]

[**Romeo** *and* **Balthazar** *appear, armed with tools and a torch*]

**Romeo**    Give me the pick and the crow-bar. Wait, take this letter: you must deliver it early in the morning to my father.

25    Give me the light. Upon thy life I charge thee,
      Whate'er thou hear'st or seest, stand all aloof
      And do not interrupt me in my course.
      Why I descend into this bed of death
      Is partly to behold my lady's face
30    But chiefly to take thence from her dead finger
      A precious ring, a ring that I must use
      In dear employment. Therefore hence, be gone.
      But if thou jealous dost return to pry
      In what I farther shall intend to do,
35    By heaven I will tear thee joint by joint,
      And strew this hungry churchyard with thy limbs.
      The time and my intents are savage-wild,
      More fierce and more inexorable far
      Than empty tigers or the roaring sea.

40  **Balthazar**    I will be gone, sir, and not trouble ye.

    **Romeo**    So shalt thou show me friendship. Take thou that.
      Live and be prosperous, and farewell, good fellow.

    **Balthazar**    For all this same, I'll hide me hereabout.
      His looks I fear, and his intents I doubt.

                                          [**Balthazar** *retires*]

45  **Romeo**    Thou detestable maw, thou womb of death
      Gorged with the dearest morsel of the earth,
      Thus I enforce thy rotten jaws to open,
      And in despite I'll cram thee with more food.

    [**Romeo** *opens the tomb*]

    **Paris**    This is that banished haughty Montague
50    That murdered my love's cousin – with which grief
      It is supposed the fair creature died –
      And here is come to do some villainous shame

236

Give me the light. Whatever you hear or see, I order you, on peril of your life, to stand apart: don't try to interrupt me in what I do. The reason I've come down into this tomb is partly to see my loved one's face, but chiefly to remove a precious ring from her dead finger, a ring that I must use in a personal matter. So go, away! If, all suspicious, you return to pry, to see what else I intend to do, by heaven, I'll tear you limb from limb, and spread the parts around this corpse-consuming churchyard! The hour and my intentions are savage – wild – fiercer and far more ruthless than hungry tigers on the roaring sea!

**Balthazar**   I'll go, sir, and not bother you!

**Romeo**   That way you'll show me friendship. [*Giving him money*] Take that; live and prosper. Farewell, good fellow!

**Balthazar**   [*to himself*] All the same, I'll hide nearby. I don't like his looks, and I suspect his intentions.

[*He hides in the churchyard*]

**Romeo**   [*Cursing the tomb as if it were human*] You loathsome stomach! You belly of death! Gorged with the dearest morsel of this earth! I'm forcing open your rotten jaws, and in revenge I'll cram you with more food! [*He means himself*]

[**Romeo** *opens the tomb*]

**Paris**   This is that banished, arrogant Montague, who murdered my beloved's cousin – from the grief of which, it's

To the dead bodies. I will apprehend him.
Stop thy unhallowed toil, vile Montague.
55  Can vengeance be pursued further than death?
Condemned villain, I do apprehend thee.
Obey, and go with me, for thou must die.

**Romeo**   I must indeed, and therefore came I hither.
Good gentle youth, tempt not a desperate man.
60  Fly hence and leave me. Think upon these gone.
Let them affright thee. I beseech thee, youth,
Put not another sin upon my head
By urging me to fury. O be gone.
By heaven I love thee better than myself,
65  For I come hither armed against myself.
Stay not, be gone, live, and hereafter say
A mad man's mercy bid thee run away.

**Paris**   I do defy thy conjuration
And apprehend thee for a felon here.

70  **Romeo**   Wilt thou provoke me? Then have at thee, boy!

[*They fight*]

**Page**   O Lord, they fight! I will go call the Watch.

[*Exit* **Page**]

**Paris**   O, I am slain! If thou be merciful,
Open the tomb, lay me with Juliet.

[**Paris** *dies*]

**Romeo**   In faith I will. Let me peruse this face.
75  Mercutio's kinsman, noble County Paris!

thought she died. He's here to desecrate the bodies. I'll arrest him.

[*He comes forward*]

Montague! Stop your devilish work! Can vengeance be pursued beyond the grave? Condemned villain! I arrest you! Do as I say, and come with me, for you must die!

**Romeo**   I must indeed, and that's why I came here. My dear boy, don't provoke a desperate man. Run away, and leave me. Give some thought to these departed. [**Romeo** *indicates the corpses in the tomb*] Be frightened by them. I beg you, young man, don't add another sin to my score by stirring me to anger. Go away! By heaven, I love you more than I love myself, and came here equipped to do myself some harm. Don't stay. Go, live, and in later years, say that it was the mercy of a madman that caused you to run away.

**Paris**   I reject your entreaties! I arrest you as an outlaw here!

**Romeo**   You insist on provoking me? Then have at you boy!

[*They fight with their swords*]

**Page**   Oh Lord! They're fighting! I'll go and bring the constables.

[*The* **Page** *goes*]

**Paris**   [*falling to the ground*] Oh, I'm killed! If you have any mercy, open the tomb and lay me beside Juliet.

[**Paris** *dies*]

**Romeo**   Indeed I will. Let me see your face. [*He examines* **Paris** *by the light of the torch*] Mercutio's relation! The noble Count

What said my man, when my betossed soul
Did not attend him, as we rode? I think
He told me Paris should have married Juliet.
Said he not so? Or did I dream it so?
80    Or am I mad, hearing him talk of Juliet,
To think it was so? O, give me thy hand,
One writ with me in sour misfortune's book.
I'll bury thee in a triumphant grave.
A grave? O no, a lantern, slaughtered youth.
85    For here lies Juliet, and her beauty makes
This vault a feasting presence, full of light.
Death, lie thou there, by a dead man interred.
How oft when men are at the point of death
Have they been merry! Which their keepers call
90    A lightning before death. O how may I
Call this a lightning? O my love, my wife,
Death that hath sucked the honey of thy breath
Hath had no power yet upon thy beauty.
Thou art not conquered. Beauty's ensign yet
95    Is crimson in thy lips and in thy cheeks,
And Death's pale flag is not advanced there.
Tybalt, liest thou there in thy bloody sheet?
O, what more favour can I do to thee
Than with that hand that cut thy youth in twain
100    To sunder his that was thine enemy?
Forgive me, cousin. Ah, dear Juliet,
Why art thou yet so fair? Shall I believe
That unsubstantial Death is amorous,
And that the lean abhorred monster keeps
105    Thee here in dark to be his paramour?
For fear of that I still will stay with thee,
And never from this palace of dim night
Depart again. Here, here, will I remain
With worms that are thy chambermaids. O here
110    Will I set up my everlasting rest

Paris! What did my servant say, when my mind was elsewhere, as we rode here? I think he told me that Paris was to have married Juliet. Wasn't that it? Or did I dream it? Or am I mad – hearing him speak of Juliet – for thinking that was it? [*He goes to pick* **Paris** *up*] Give me your hand: like me, your name is written in the Book of Misfortune. I'll bury you in a splendid grave. A grave? Oh, no: a palace, slaughtered youth. Juliet lies here, and her beauty makes this vault a banquet hall, full of light. Death [*he refers to* **Paris**] lie there. [*He puts the body down by* **Juliet**] Buried by a dead man! [*Again, he means himself*] How often, when men are at the point of death, they feel elated! Their gaolers call it 'a lightning'. How could I call this [*looking round the gloomy vault*] a lightning? [*To* **Juliet**] Oh, my love! my wife! Death, that has taken your sweet breath, has no power over your beauty. You aren't conquered yet. Your lips and cheeks are red, emblems of your beauty: death has not raised its pale flag of victory over them. [*He turns to look at* **Tybalt**] Tybalt! Is that you, lying there in your blood-stained shroud? What better favour can I do for you than use the selfsame hand that cut your life so short, to end the one belonging to your enemy? Forgive me, friend. [*He returns to* **Juliet**] Ah, dear Juliet: why are you still so beautiful? Am I to understand that shadowy Death is lecherous, and that the famished and repulsive monster is keeping you here secretly, to be his mistress? For fear of that, I'll stay with you forever, and never leave this palace of dim night again. Here, here I shall remain, with worms my chambermaids. Here I'll set myself up for eternity, and never

And shake the yoke of inauspicious stars
From this world-wearied flesh. Eyes, look your last.
Arms, take your last embrace! And lips, O you
The doors of breath, seal with a righteous kiss
115   A dateless bargain to engrossing Death.
Come, bitter conduct, come unsavoury guide,
Thou desperate pilot now at once run on
The dashing rocks thy seasick weary bark.
Here's to my love! [*He drinks*] O true apothecary,
120   Thy drugs are quick. Thus with a kiss I die.

[*He falls*]

[*Enter* **Friar Lawrence** *with lantern, crow and spade*]

**Friar Lawrence**   Saint Francis be my speed. How oft tonight
Have my old feet stumbled at graves. Who's there?

**Balthazar**   Here's one, a friend, and one that knows you well.

**Friar Lawrence**   Bliss be upon you. Tell me, good my friend,
125   What torch is yond that vainly lends his light
To grubs and eyeless skulls? As I discern,
It burneth in the Capels' monument.

**Balthazar**   It doth so, holy sir, and there's my master,
One that you love

**Friar Lawrence**      Who is it?

130 **Balthazar**              Romeo.

**Friar Lawrence**   How long hath he been there?

**Balthazar**                Full half an hour.

**Friar Lawrence**   Go with me to the vault.

more will my world-weary body suffer from the burden of unfavourable stars. Eyes, see, for the last time. Arms – [*he holds* **Juliet** *to him*] enjoy your last embrace! And lips – you doors of breath – seal with a virtuous kiss an everlasting contract with all-claiming Death. [*He raises the poison bottle to his mouth*] Come, you bitter escort; come, distasteful guide; you imperilled pilot, with your ship weary of its travel, and now dashed upon the rocks. Here's to my love! [*He drinks the poison*] Oh, honest chemist! Your drugs are quick. [*His head falls on* **Juliet***'s*] With a kiss, I die.

[**Romeo** *dies*]

[*Enter* **Friar Lawrence,** *with a lantern and equipment, at the door of the tomb*]

**Friar Lawrence**    St Francis speed me! How often tonight have my old feet stumbled over graves! Who's here?

[*He lifts his light to see*]

**Balthazar**    A friend, who knows you well.

**Friar Lawrence**    Bliss be yours. Tell me, my good friend, whose light is that over there, which seems to be wasted on worms and skeletons? It looks as if it's burning in the vault of the Capulets.

**Balthazar**    It does, holy sir. My master's there – one you love.

**Friar Lawrence**    Who's that?

**Balthazar**    Romeo.

**Friar Lawrence**    How long has he been there?

**Balthazar**    Fully half an hour.

**Friar Lawrence**    Come with me to the vault.

**Balthazar**                                    I dare not, sir.
My master knows not but I am gone hence,
And fearfully did menace me with death
If I did stay to look on his intents.

135 **Friar Lawrence**    Stay then, I'll go alone. Fear comes upon me.
O, much I fear some ill unthrifty thing.

**Balthazar**    As I did sleep under this yew tree here
I dreamt my master and another fought,
And that my master slew him.

**Friar Lawrence**                        Romeo!

[**Friar Lawrence** *stoops and looks on the blood and weapons*]

140    Alack, alack, what blood is this which stains
The stony entrance of this sepulchre?
What means these masterless and gory swords
To lie discoloured by this place of peace?
Romeo! O, pale! Who else? What, Paris too?
145    And steeped in blood? Ah what an unkind hour
Is guilty of this lamentable chance?
The lady stirs.

[**Juliet** *rises*]

**Juliet**    O comfortable Friar, where is my lord?
I do remember well where I should be,
150    And there I am. Where is my Romeo?

**Friar Lawrence**    I hear some noise. Lady, come from that nest
Of death, contagion, and unnatural sleep.
A greater power than we can contradict
Hath thwarted our intents. Come, come away.
155    Thy husband in thy bosom there lies dead,
And Paris too. Come, I'll dispose of thee

**Balthazar**   I daren't sir. My master thinks I've gone, and he threatened me most fearfully with death if I stayed to watch his doings.

**Friar Lawrence**   Stay here, then. I'll go alone. Fear strikes me: I'm afraid something unfortunate may have happened.

**Balthazar**   As I slept under this yew tree here, I dreamt my master and someone else had a fight, and that my master killed him.

**Friar Lawrence**   Romeo! Alas, alack! Whose bloodstains are these on the stones leading to the entrance of the vault? Why are these abandoned and bloodstained swords lying near this place of peace?

[*He goes into the vault*]

Romeo! Oh, so pale! Who else? What – Paris, too? And covered in blood? What evil hour is responsible for this terrible coincidence [**Juliet** *wakens*] The lady moves . . .

**Juliet**   Oh, comforting Friar! Where is my husband? I well remember where I should be – and here I am. Where is my Romeo?

[*Voices are heard in the distance*]

**Friar Lawrence**   I can hear a noise, lady. Leave that place of death, disease, and never-ending sleep. God has intervened. Come, come away. Your husband lies dead in your arms. And Paris is dead, too. Come, I'll arrange for you to live in a

Among a sisterhood of holy nuns.
Stay not to question, for the Watch is coming.
Come, go, good Juliet. I dare no longer stay.

160 **Juliet**    Go get thee hence, for I will not away.

[*Exit* **Friar Lawrence**]

What's here? A cup closed in my true love's hand?
Poison, I see, hath been his timeless end.
O churl. Drunk all, and left no friendly drop
To help me after? I will kiss thy lips.
165 Haply some poison yet doth hang on them.
To make me die with a restorative. [*She kisses him*]
Thy lips are warm!

**Watchman**    [*Outside*]    Lead, boy. Which way?

**Juliet**    Yea, noise? Then I'll be brief. O happy dagger.
This is thy sheath. There rust, and let me die.

[*She stabs herself and falls*]

[*Enter* **Page** *and* **Watchmen**]

170 **Page**    This is the place. There, where the torch doth burn.

**First Watchman**    The ground is bloody. Search about the
churchyard.
Go, some of you: whoe'er you find, attach.

[*Exeunt some* **Watchmen**]

Pitiful sight! Here lies the County slain
175 And Juliet bleeding, warm, and newly dead,
Who here hath lain this two days buried.
Go tell the Prince. Run to the Capulets.

convent. Don't argue, the constables are coming. Come – go
with me, good Juliet. I daren't stay longer.

**Juliet**   Go, go. I'm staying here.

[**Friar Lawrence** *hurries off*]

What's this? [*She sees the poison bottle*] A container in my
true love's hand? Poison has brought him to an untimely end.
Oh, you're mean! Have you drunk it all, and left no obliging
drop to help me to follow you? I'll kiss your lips. Perhaps
there's still some poison on them, to make me die with
restoring medicine. [*She kisses him*] Your lips are warm!

[*The* **Page** *and the* **Constables** *approach the vault*]

**First Constable**   Lead the way, boy. Which way?

**Juliet**   Noise? Then I'll be quick. [*She takes Romeo's dagger*]
Oh, lucky dagger! [*She holds it to her breast*] This is your
sheath. Rust there, and let me die.

[*She stabs herself, falls on* **Romeo**, *and dies*]

[*The* **Page** *and the* **Constables** *enter the vault*]

**Page**   This is the place. There, where the torch is burning.

**First Constable**   There's blood on the ground. Search around
the churchyard. Go, some of you. Anyone you find, arrest.

[*Several* **Constables** *go out*]

A touching sight! Here lies the Count Paris, killed. And Juliet
bleeding – warm and newly dead, who's been buried here
these past two days. Go and tell the Prince. Run to the

Raise up the Montagues. Some others search.

[*Exeunt some* **Watchmen**]

We see the ground whereon these woes do lie,
180    But the true ground of all these piteous woes
We cannot without circumstance descry.

[*Enter several* **Watchmen** *with* **Balthazar**]

**Second Watchman**    Here's Romeo's man. We found him in
the churchyard.

**First Watchman**    Hold him in safety till the Prince come
185    hither.

[*Enter another* **Watchman** *with* **Friar Lawrence**]

**Third Watchman**    Here is a friar that trembles, sighs and
weeps.
We took this mattock and this spade from him
As he was coming from this churchyard's side.

190   **First Watchman**    A great suspicion. Stay the friar too.

[*Enter the* **Prince** *and Attendants*]

**Prince**    What misadventure is so early up,
That calls our person from our morning rest?

[*Enter* **Capulet** *and* **Lady Capulet** *and Servants*]

**Capulet**    What should it be that is so shrieked abroad?

**Lady Capulet**    O, the people in the street cry 'Romeo',
195    Some 'Juliet', and some 'Paris', and all run
With open outcry toward our monument.

Capulets. Awaken the Montagues. The rest, search round. [*His men obey the orders*] We see the ground on which these bodies lie. Without more information we can't determine the real grounds for their tragic end.

[*Several* **Constables** *return, with* **Balthazar**]

**Second Constable**   Here's Romeo's servant. We found him in the churchyard.

**First Constable**   Keep him safe till the Prince comes here.

[*Another* **Constable** *returns with* **Friar Lawrence**]

**Third Constable**   Here's a Friar – trembling, sighing, weeping. We took this pickaxe and spade from him as he was coming from this side of the churchyard.

**First Constable**   Very suspicious! Detain the Friar, too.

[**Prince Escalus** *and attendants arrive*]

**Prince**   What's happened to get us out of bed so early?

[**Capulet** *and* **Lady Capulet** *enter with their servants*]

**Capulet**   What's everyone shouting about?

**Lady Capulet**   Some people in the streets are crying 'Romeo!', some 'Juliet!' and some 'Paris'. They're all running towards our vault, shouting.

**Prince**    What fear is this which startles in our ears?

**First Watchman**    Sovereign, here lies the County Paris slain,
And Romeo dead, and Juliet, dead before,
200    Warm, and new killed.

**Prince**    Search, seek, and know how this foul murder comes.

**First Watchman**    Here is a friar, and slaughtered Romeo's
man,
With instruments upon them fit to open
205    These dead men's tombs.

**Capulet**    O heavens! O wife, look how our daughter bleeds!
This dagger hath mista'en, for lo, his house
Is empty on the back of Montague,
And it mis-sheathed in my daughter's bosom.

210    **Lady Capulet**    O me! This sight of death is as a bell
That warns my old age to a sepulchre.

[*Enter* **Montague** *and Servants*]

**Prince**    Come, Montague, for thou art early up
To see thy son and heir now early down.

**Montague**    Alas, my liege, my wife is dead tonight.
215    Grief of my son's exile hath stopped her breath.
What further woe conspires against mine age?

**Prince**    Look and thou shalt see.

**Montague**    O thou untaught! What manners is in this,
To press before thy father to a grave?

220    **Prince**    Seal up the mouth of outrage for a while
Till we can clear these ambiguities
And know their spring, their head, their true descent,
And then will I be general of your woes

**Prince**    What's upsetting you all?

**First Constable**    Your majesty: here's the Count Paris, killed. And Romeo, dead. And Juliet, dead once before, still warm and newly killed.

**Prince**    Make full enquiries as to how this foul murder has come about!

**First Constable**    Here is a Friar, and Romeo's servant, with tools on them to open tombs like these.

**Capulet**    Oh, heavens! Oh, wife! See how our daughter is bleeding. This dagger has lost its way. It should be in that Montague's back, not in my daughter's bosom!

**Lady Capulet**    Alas, seeing death like this warns me that my own time is near.

[**Montague** *enters*]

**Prince**    Come now, Montague: you are up early to see your son and heir untimely down.

**Montague**    Alas, my lord, my wife died last night, heartbroken at my son's exile. What further calamity threatens my old age?

**Prince**    See for yourself.

**Montague**    [*to* **Romeo,** *with wry irony*] Such impoliteness! What bad manners is this, to push ahead of your father to the grave?

**Prince**    Staunch your grief for now, till we can clear these puzzles up, and find their source, their fountain-head, and their natural course. Then I'll lead you in mourning, even as far

And lead you, even to death. Meantime forbear,
225 And let mischance be slave to patience.
Bring forth the parties of suspicion.

**Friar Lawrence**    I am the greatest, able to do least,
Yet most suspected, as the time and place
Doth make against me, of this direful murder.
230 And here I stand, both to impeach and purge
Myself condemned and myself excused.

**Prince**    Then say at once what thou dost know in this.

**Friar Lawrence**    I will be brief, for my short date of breath
Is not so long as is a tedious tale.
235 Romeo, there dead, was husband to that Juliet,
And she, there dead, that Romeo's faithful wife.
I married them, and their stol'n marriage day
Was Tybalt's doomsday, whose untimely death
Banished the new-made bridegroom from this city;
240 For whom, and not for Tybalt, Juliet pined.
You, to remove that siege of grief from her,
Betrothed and would have married her perforce
To County Paris. Then comes she to me
And with wild looks bid me devise some mean
245 To rid her from this second marriage,
Or in my cell there would she kill herself.
Then gave I her – so tutored by my art –
A sleeping potion, which so took effect
As I intended, for it wrought on her
250 The form of death. Meantime I writ to Romeo
That he should hither come as this dire night
To help to take her from her borrowed grave,
Being the time the potion's force should cease.
But he which bore my letter, Friar John,
255 Was stayed by accident, and yesternight
Returned my letter back. Then all alone

as death. Meanwhile, control your grief. Submit patiently to misfortune. [*To the* **Constables**] Bring the suspects forward.

[**Friar Lawrence** *and* **Balthazar** *are presented to the* **Prince**]

**Friar Lawrence**    I'm the senior one: the most powerless, yet most suspected – because of circumstantial evidence – of this dreadful murder. Here I stand, both to accuse, and to clear my name. Condemned by myself, and by myself proved innocent.

**Prince**    Then say what you know about this, immediately!

**Friar Lawrence**    I shall be brief, because I won't live long enough to tell a lengthy tale. Romeo, who lies dead there, was the husband of that Juliet. She, also dead, was the faithful wife of Romeo there. I married them. Their secret marriage day was also Tybalt's last. His untimely death resulted in the bridegroom's banishment from this city. It was for him, not Tybalt, that Juliet pined. [*To* **Capulet**] You would have married her by force to Count Paris, to end her grief. Then she came to me, and distractedly asked me to devise some means to save her from this second marriage, saying she would otherwise kill herself there in my cell. Then I gave her a sleeping potion; I have such skills. It produced the expected effect: it gave her the appearance of death. Meanwhile, I wrote to Romeo, telling him to come here tonight to help to take her from her temporary grave, that being the time when the potion should wear off. But Friar John, who carried the letter, was delayed accidentally, and last night he gave me the letter back. Then,

At the prefixed hour of her waking
Came I to take her from her kindred's vault,
Meaning to keep her closely at my cell
260 Till I conveniently could send to Romeo.
But when I came, some minute ere the time
Of her awakening, here untimely lay
The noble Paris and true Romeo dead.
She wakes, and I entreated her come forth
265 And bear this work of heaven with patience,
But then a noise did scare me from the tomb
And she, too desperate, would not go with me
But, as it seems, did violence on herself.
All this I know; and to the marriage
270 Her Nurse is privy; and if aught in this
Miscarried by my fault, let my old life
Be sacrificed some hour before his time
Unto the rigour of severest law.

**Prince**   We still have known thee for a holy man.
275 Where's Romeo's man? What can he say to this?

**Balthazar**   I brought my master news of Juliet's death,
And then in post he came from Mantua
To this same place, to this same monument.
This letter he early bid me give his father
280 And threatened me with death, going in the vault,
If I departed not and left him there.

**Prince**   Give me the letter, I will look on it.
Where is the County's Page that raised the Watch?
Sirrah, what made your master in this place?

285 **Page**   He came with flowers to strew his lady's grave
And bid me stand aloof, and so I did.
Anon comes one with light to ope the tomb
And by and by my master drew on him,
And then I ran away to call the Watch.

by myself, at the pre-arranged time of her awakening, I came to
take her from her family vault, intending to keep her hidden at
my cell till I could conveniently send a message to Romeo. But
when I arrived, a few minutes before she was due to waken I
found the noble Paris and faithful Romeo dead. She woke;
and I begged her to leave, and bear God's will with patience.
But then a noise scared me away from the tomb, and she, too
overwrought, would not go with me. It would seem that she
committed suicide. This is all I know. Her Nurse knows all
about the marriage. If anything in all this mischanced through
a fault of mine, may my old life be taken before its time,
according to the utmost rigour of the law.

**Prince**   We've always known you to be a holy man. Where's
Romeo's servant? What can he add to this?

**Balthazar**   I took news of Juliet's death to my master. Then,
post-haste, he returned from Mantua to here, this very tomb.
He told me to give this letter to his father as soon as possible,
and threatened me with death, as he was entering the vault, if I
didn't go, and leave him there.

**Prince**   Give me the letter. I'll read it. Where is the Count's Page,
who called the constables?

[*The* **Page** *steps forward*]

Now, sir: what was your master doing in this place?

**Page**   He came with flowers to strew on his lady's grave, and
told me to keep at a distance, and so I did. Soon, someone
came with a torch, to open the tomb, and then my master
drew on him, and then I ran away to call the constables.

290   **Prince**   This letter doth make good the Friar's words:
      Their course of love, the tidings of her death,
      And here he writes that he did buy a poison
      Of a poor pothecary, and therewithal
      Came to this vault to die and lie with Juliet.
295   Where be these enemies? Capulet, Montague,
      See what a scourge is laid upon your hate,
      That heaven finds means to kill your joys with love;
      And I, for winking at your discords too,
      Have lost a brace of kinsmen. All are punished.

300   **Capulet**   O brother Montague, give me thy hand.
      This is my daughter's jointure, for no more
      Can I demand.

      **Montague**          But I can give thee more,
      For I will raise her statue in pure gold,
      That whiles Verona by that name is known,
305   There shall no figure at such rate be set
      As that of true and faithful Juliet.

      **Capulet**   As rich shall Romeo's by his lady's lie,
      Poor sacrifices of our enmity.

      **Prince**   A glooming peace this morning with it brings.
310   The sun for sorrow will not show his head.
      Go hence to have more talk of these sad things.
      Some shall be pardoned, and some punished,
      For never was a story of more woe
      Than this of Juliet and her Romeo.

                                        [*Exeunt*]

**Prince**    [*scanning the letter*] This letter confirms the Friar's words; the course of their love, the news of her death. And here he writes that he bought the poison from an impoverished chemist, and came with it to this vault to die, and lie, with Juliet. [*He looks up*] Where are the two enemies, Capulet and Montague? [*They come before him*] See how your hate is punished: God has found a way to kill your children through love. And I have lost two relatives through turning a blind eye to your quarrels. We are all punished.

**Capulet**    Montague, my brother: shake hands. This is my daughter's wedding gift from you: I can ask no more.

**Montague**    I can give you more. I'll have a statue made of her in solid gold, so that while there is ever a Verona, no one shall surpass in value and in reputation the true and faithful Juliet.

**Capulet**    As rich a one of Romeo I'll place by his wife's side. They are the unfortunate victims of our enmity.

**Prince**    Morning has brought with it a melancholy kind of peace: the sun, in sorrow, will not show its face. Go now and talk more fully about these sad events. Some shall be pardoned. Others punished. There never was a more tragic story than that of Juliet and her Romeo.

[*They all leave*]

# Activities

## Characters

Search the original text to find answers to the following questions. They will help you to form personal opinions about the major characters in the play. *Record any relevant quotations in Shakespeare's own words.*

### Romeo

1 Which six adjectives used by the Chorus in the *Prologue* to *Act I* reveal the tragic nature of the part Romeo is to play?

2 From Benvolio's description in *Act I Scene 1* of Romeo's behaviour, and his father's confirmation of it, list four of the characteristics of a young man in love.

3 Which of the first twelve lines spoken by Romeo sum up the theme of the play as a whole?

4 The typical Elizabethan lover was (i) melancholy (ii) contemplative (iii) given to idealism (iv) tortured (v) in love with perfection and (vi) in love with love.
   Find examples from *Act I Scene 1* that suggest Romeo at this stage is a typical Elizabethan lover.

5 In *Act I Scene 4* Romeo says that he 'dreamt a dream', but gives us no details of it.
   a What clue does he give us towards the end of the scene as to its ominous nature?
   b Where else in the play does Romeo tell us that he has been dreaming?

6 In *Act I Scene 5* Romeo sees Juliet for the first time, and

admires her from a distance. Which of his words in *Act I Scene 2* are thereby contradicted?

7   Which words of Capulet in *Act I Scene 5* add to our understanding of Romeo's character?

8   Romeo's first words to Juliet, and her replies, are written in sonnet form. Identify the beginning and end of the sonnet, and explain why Shakespeare chose this point to introduce it. What do you notice about the use of verse elsewhere in the scene?

9   The Chorus opens *Act II* with a sonnet in which a distinction is made between Romeo's relationship with Rosaline, and his love-affair with Juliet. What is the big difference?

10  After this introductory sonnet, Shakespeare uses rhyme sparingly. Romeo and Juliet's love scene (*Act II Scene 2*) is mostly in blank verse. How does this emphasize the difference between the old Romeo and the new one who has fallen in love with Juliet?

11  In this edition of the play, the first six lines of *Act II Scene 3* are ascribed to Friar Lawrence, partly because they are in rhyming couplets like the rest of this scene. In some editions, they are given to Romeo as the closing lines of *Act II Scene 2*, because they seem appropriate to his mood and character. Which do you think Shakespeare intended?

12  In *Act II Scene 3*, Friar Lawrence distinguishes between the two forms of love experienced by Romeo, and says that Rosaline wisely recognised the difference between them. Find the words which confirm this.

13  What new aspect of Romeo's character is demonstrated in *Act II Scene 4*?

14  How does Romeo's treatment of the Nurse in *Act 2 Scene 4*, in differing from that of Mercutio, bear out the kind remarks of Capulet about him in *Act I Scene 5*?

15 The first lines Romeo speaks in *Act II Scene 6* are profoundly related to the tragedy of his love for Juliet.
   a Explain why
   b Comment on Friar Lawrence's predictions in reply.

16 Two opposing aspects of Romeo's character are shown in *Act III Scene 1*. What are they? Which speech of Benvolio's describes both?

17 Friar Lawrence breaks the news to Romeo of his banishment in *Act III Scene 3*. Consider Romeo's reactions in terms of his words, deeds, and response to Lawrence's 'good counsel'.

18 Compare Romeo's behaviour in *Act III Scene 3* with that of *Act V Scene 1*, when his servant reports the death of Juliet. How has his character developed?

19 In *Act V Scene 3* Romeo refers to himself as 'a desperate man'.
   a What does he do and say that bears this out?
   b Why do you think Paris speaks in rhyming verse in that scene, whereas Romeo uses blank verse?

20 In his last speech, Romeo says that he is 'writ . . . in sour misfortune's book'. How many occasions can you trace of Romeo's fortune being influenced by coincidence and fate?

## Juliet

1 What words of Juliet's in *Act I Scene 3*
   a stress her youthful sense of obedience
   b hint at the mature strength she is to show later?
   How do the Nurse's reminiscences in the scene help to focus on the Juliet of the immediate present, and the Juliet of the future?

2 a In *Act I Scene 5*, Juliet shares with Romeo a dialogue in sonnet form. Identify it, and show how their love-affair makes physical progress through Juliet's adept responses to Romeo's purposeful advances.

   b Which of her remarks after Romeo leaves is ominously prophetic?

3  a How does Juliet answer the theoretical charge of 'yielding to light love' in *Act II Scene 2*, and thereby establish her sincerity?

   b In the same scene, which of her words show that in spite of losing her heart, she has not entirely lost her head?

4  Juliet's 'three words' in *Act II Scene 2* to the departing Romeo begin a series of amusing and engaging stratagems that typify young, innocent love. Identify them.

5  In *Act II Scene 2*, Juliet finds time too short. In *Act II Scene 5*, she finds it is too long. What other example can you find of Juliet's impetuosity?

6  Juliet says that old people are 'unwieldy, slow, heavy, pale as lead'. Examine her handling of the Nurse in *Act II Scene 5*, and comment on her qualities of self-control.

7  Juliet's soliloquy at the beginning of *Act III Scene 2* was often omitted as being too indelicate for actresses to perform. Today, it is regarded as a central speech.

   a How does it mark an important progression in Juliet's relationship with Romeo?

   b How does Juliet convey strength and determination in her use of words?

8  The rest of *Act III Scene 2* shows Juliet under strain.

   a Show how the news brought by the Nurse produces in her an agonizing division of loyalties.

   b Which of her words point to the tragic ending that is to come?

9  In *Act III Scene 5*, Juliet is seen as both wife and daughter.

   a *As wife*, how is her innocence and womanliness conveyed in the context of dawn's approach?

   b Which of her parting words to Romeo foreshadow what is to come?

   c *As daughter*, how does she cleverly play the role expected of her by her mother?

d Which words show that Juliet has a fiery spirit?

10 Juliet is not equal to her father's anger in *Act III Scene 5*, but by the end of the scene she is wiser and more determined. What part does the Nurse play in this development?

11 a How does Juliet's handling of the encounter with Paris at Friar Lawrence's cell (*Act IV Scene 1*) show that she is developing and maturing in her ability to handle situations?

   b How does her discussion with Friar Lawrence confirm that she has courage and resolution?

12 In *Act IV Scene 2*, Juliet shows further evidence of her growing maturity. Show how she manipulates her father and the Nurse to gain her objectives.

13 In *Act IV Scene 3* Juliet almost returns to the safety of childhood when she calls for the Nurse to return, but she quickly realizes that she 'must act alone'. Show how Juliet's speech before drinking the potion is evidence of her awareness of the ordeal before her.

14 Juliet's death in *Act V Scene 3* by means of Romeo's dagger is a swift answer to Friar Lawrence's option of a life 'among a sisterhood of nuns'. On what occasion had Juliet considered suicide before?

15 In the closing lines of the play, the 'woe' is said to be that of 'Juliet and her Romeo'. Is there a distinction to be made between the suffering of the two lovers, and should Juliet's name be given precedence?

## Mercutio

1 In *Act I Scene 4*, Mercutio's bright spirits contrast with Romeo's melancholy.

   a What is Mercutio's recommended cure for love?

   b What is his attitude to dreams?

How does the Queen Mab speech demonstrate vividly, memorably and imaginatively his contention that 'dreamers often lie'?

2 What examples are there in this scene of Mercutio's
a delight in wordplay
b flair for bawdy repartee
c self-mockery
d concern for a friend?
Is Romeo right in saying of Mercutio 'thou talkest of nothing'?

3 Mercutio's wit takes a literary turn in *Act II Scene 1*. What style of poetry is he mocking here?
a Is Romeo indeed guilty of its worst excesses during his Rosaline period?
b Is Romeo's rebuke at the opening of *Act II Scene 2* justified?

4 Mercutio further develops his attack on affectation in *Act II Scene 4*.
a How does he mock Tybalt's affected fencing style?
b How does he mock affectations of speech?
c How does he mock affectations of dress?

5 Word duels are now out of fashion, but Mercutio competes with Romeo for a deliberate purpose: to drive away his melancholy. Which speech confirms this in *Act II Scene 4*?

6 Mercutio has no respect for age or sex. Illustrate his irreverence by reference to his dialogue with the Nurse at the end of *Act II Scene 4*.

7 In *Act III Scene 1*, Mercutio's opening target is Benvolio. Do you think he intends his accusations to be taken seriously, or are they an outrageous jest?

8 The encounter with Tybalt is first acted out, then reported on by Benvolio. In what way is Benvolio's account biased in Mercutio's favour?

9 In what ways does Mercutio die as he lived?

10 Mercutio's dying words put the blame for his death on the feuding Capulets and Montagues. Does this bear the kind of critical examination Mercutio practised on others?

## The Nurse

1 The Nurse's first words in *Act I Scene 3* show her to be (i) coarse (ii) loving and (iii) caring.

Explain and demonstrate how so much can be conveyed so economically.

2 Show how the Nurse's comic qualities in this scene include (i) garrulity (ii) insensitivity (iii) a tendency to repetition (iv) an interest in fine detail and (v) a simple though bawdy sense of humour.

How would you describe her relationship with her employers? (There is further relevant information in *Act III Scene 5*, and *Act IV Scene 4*.)

3 The Nurse is subject to mockery and ribaldry in *Act II Scene 4*.

a What is the target of Romeo's wit?

b How does Mercutio tease her?

c Which of her weaknesses does Benvolio satirize?

d What is amusing about her expressions of indignation when talking to Romeo privately?

e How do we know she is illiterate?

f What story does she nearly tell Romeo that we have heard before?

g What does her manner with Peter tell us of her character?

4 In *Act II Scene 5* the Nurse makes the most of her advantage over Juliet, by procrastinating.

   (i) a What is the Nurse's first teasing trick?

      b What is the first ailment she complains of?

      c What is the second?

      d The third?
      e The fourth?
  (ii) How does she use
      a irrelevant questions?
      b digressions?
      c provocative remarks?
      d 'coil'?
 (iii) Do you think her role as go-between ('I am the drudge, and toil in your delight') is
      a excusable because she wants Juliet to be happy, or
      b inexcusable, because she is party to deceit?

5 'What devil art thou that dost torment me thus?' Juliet complains, in *Act III Scene 2*.
  a In this case, do you think the Nurse is playing games, or
  b is the priority she gives to Tybalt's death a reasonable one in the circumstances?
  What evidence is there in support of the latter interpretation?

6 In *Act III Scene 5*, the Nurse first defends Juliet in spite of Capulet's wrath, then offers advice which ends her role as a confidante. Consider what Juliet says at the end of the scene. Is it justified?

## Friar Lawrence

1 The Friar first appears in *Act II Scene 3*: his opening soliloquy tells us why he is collecting 'baleful weeds and precious-juiced flowers'.
  a How does his speech, with its homely truths, relate to Romeo's suicide?
  b Which two lines of this opening homily could be cited to explain why the Friar agrees to marry the two young lovers?

2  What is ominous about the Friar's opening and subsequent words on the occasion when we next meet him (*Act II Scene 6*)?

3  In *Act III Scene 3* the Friar performs a number of tasks for Romeo:
   a  He breaks the news of banishment. How does he handle Romeo's emotional reaction?
   b  He prevents him from attempting suicide. What are the arguments he uses?
   c  He organizes Romeo's immediate future. How do Romeo and the Nurse react?

4  In *Act IV Scene 1*, the Friar acts in a similar way with Juliet, diverting her from thoughts of suicide and providing her with a plan of action. How does this further involve the Friar in terms of
   a  his dealings with the Capulet family
   b  his dealings with Friar John
   c  his obligations at the Capulet vault?
   His final offer of help is rejected. What is it?

5  At the conclusion of his explanatory speech in *Act V Scene 3*, the Friar says 'If aught in this / Miscarried by my fault, let my old life be sacrificed. . . .' Read his account carefully, and decide whether you would find him guilty of any misdemeanour.

## Paris

1  The first we see of Paris is in *Act I Scene 2*. What is different about Paris's approach to Juliet compared with Romeo's?

2  The next we see of him is in *Act III Scene 4*.
   a  How does Capulet confirm that Paris and Romeo have wooed Juliet in different ways?
   b  What does he instruct his wife to do which emphasizes the difference?

3    The first time Paris and Juliet are seen together is in *Act IV Scene 1*

    a What is notable about his speeches to her, and her replies?

    b How does the manner of his kissing Juliet for the first time compare with that of Romeo in *Act I Scene 5*?

4    The first time Paris meets Romeo is in *Act V Scene 3*, in the Capulet vault.

    a Paris tries to arrest his rival rather than fight him: how might this be said to be consistent with his behaviour and character as we have known it throughout the play?

    b How do the dying words of Paris confirm that his love for Juliet, and his words over her body, were sincere?

# Close reading

The following questions refer to the original text:

1 *'Two households, both alike in dignity'* (*Act I: The Prologue*)

  (i) This is an Elizabethan sonnet. How many syllables are there in each line?

  (ii) A Shakespearian sonnet rhymes abab cdcd efef gg. A quatrain is a group of four lines; a couplet, two.

    a Explain how how each quatrain has a unity, by examining the content carefully.

    b What might have been the practical purpose of the couplet in performance?

    c Choose six adjectives that prepare the audience for a tragic play. Which of these involve Fate?

    d Why do you think Shakespeare avoided figurative language?

    e In classical drama, the Chorus consisted of several characters speaking in unison. When Shakespeare employs a Chorus, it is always one man. What dramatic advantage does he gain here by the simpler form?

2 *'Now old desire doth in his deathbed lie'* (*Act II: The Prologue*)

There is no new information in this sonnet; some critics have said it is superfluous, and it does not appear in the First Quarto edition.

  a What do you think it achieves from the point of view of the playgoer whose attention must be held for at least two hours?

  b The key words of the Chorus's first sonnet are ominous and austere. His second sonnet has a lighter tone. Which words establish this?

**3** *'If I profane with my unworthiest hand'* (Act I Scene 5)

a This sonnet forms part of the dialogue. How does its rhyming scheme differ from the previous sonnets?

b Which words establish the religious base of the argument and the figures of speech?

c How is the sonnet divided between Romeo and Juliet so as to suggest that a verbal duel is being fought out?

d Romeo begins the first quatrain with a supposition: 'If'. He ends it with a firm proposal. Explain how he uses figurative language to achieve his objective.

e Juliet's reply is witty – and modest, in that she deflects his proposal and withholds the requested kiss. Explain her argument.

f In the third quatrain, the duel quickens up; question, answer, proposal again. Trace the ingenious logic.

g The final couplet is shared; one line is Juliet's, and the other Romeo's. What is the verb common to both which enables Romeo to achieve his objective in a formal and logical way?

**4** *'Read o'er the volume of young Paris' face'* (Act I Scene 3)

a This is a sustained metaphor. How many variations on the 'volume' theme can you identify?

b The speech is built on rhyming couplets. Do you think the embellishment of rhyme (i) gives the passage distinction or (ii) emphasizes its formality and artificiality: or both?

c The line that follows (spoken by the Nurse) is coarse and unromantic. Lady Capulet deliberately ignores it. What was Shakespeare's purpose in writing it?

**5** *'Even or odd, of all days in the year'* (Act I Scene 3)

a In the Second Quarto (the one which replaced the printed version of 1597) this speech is printed as prose, the usual vehicle for characters belonging to the lower orders. It is now mostly printed in verse. Which do you (i) prefer; (ii) think Shakespeare intended?

b The Nurse easily digresses: find some examples.

c She speaks in clichés: make a list of them.

d She uses expletives: how many can you find?

e She remembers small details: which interrupt the narrative?

f She repeats herself: what is the outstanding example here?

6 *'O then, I see Queen Mab hath been with you'* (Act I Scene 4)

a This is a brilliant set speech, but it is a response to a remark of Romeo's about the wisdom of attending the masque. Romeo returns to the same theme (which the Queen Mab speech interrupts) at the end of the scene. Find these two passages to place Mercutio's speech in context.

b How does Mercutio establish Mab's extreme smallness in the lines which conclude with 'And in this state'?

c Mab seems to get bigger as Mercutio warms up. Which roles require her to enlarge in size?

d List the dreamers said to be visited by Mab during sleep. How are their dreams related to their work or interests?

e The pace of the speech quickens, too, as Mercutio begins a new phase in his descriptions. Where does that phase begin, and why do you think Romeo cuts him short?

f Which words used by Mercutio make dreams seem light and insubstantial?

7 *'Romeo, Romeo, wherefore art thou Romeo?'* (Act II Scene 2)

These words and those in the speech which follow are some of the most memorable Shakespeare ever wrote.
Account for this.

**8** '*The grey-ey'd morn smiles on the frowning night*' (*Act II Scene 3*)

a The first four lines of Friar Lawrence's speech are some-times attributed to Romeo, as part of his final words in *Act II Scene 2*. Read these carefully. Which seems to you to be what Shakespeare intended?

b The speech is a soliloquy, and in couplets. Why is rhyme appropriate to the sentiments the Friar is expressing?

c What is the connection between what he is saying and the play as a whole?

**9** '*Gallop apace, you fiery-footed steeds*' (*Act III Scene 2*)

a Phoebus (Greek for 'the shining one') was the sun-god. Phaeton was his son. According to mythology, Phaeton drove his father's chariot recklessly, and almost set the world on fire. Which words in the soliloquy stress speed and haste?

b What metaphorical references are made to Night? How are these appropriate to Juliet's mood?

c The words 'that runaway's eyes may wink' have puzzled editors and we can only conjecture as to Shakespeare's meaning. The 'runaway' could be the sun, chased by night. 'Runaway' could refer to night itself, with its stars that 'wink'. The word could be plural, and 'runaways', people like Romeo and Juliet who have eloped. Cupid is often referred to as 'a runaway'. Which meaning do you think makes most sense?

d Hawks are hooded to keep them calm during training. How does the image relate to Juliet in the circumstances of this speech?

e 'When he shall die' is sometimes printed as 'When I shall die'. Which seems to you to make the better sense in this context, and why?

f  Juliet's metaphor – 'O, I have bought the mansion of a love . . .' – is followed through with reference to a sale. Is the reversal a slip on Shakespeare's part, or do you think it is intended to convey Juliet's mental excitement?

**10**  *'In faith I will. Let me peruse this face'* (**Romeo**)

*'What's here? A cup closed in my true love's hand?'* (**Juliet**)

(*Act V Scene 3*)

a  These two soliloquies are death-speeches. They differ greatly in length. What dramatic justification is there for this?

b  Romeo first talks about Paris, his rival, whom he has killed. From the way he speaks, what do we learn of his state of mind?

c  When Romeo turns to Juliet, darkness gives way to light: how does Shakespeare suggest Juliet's radiance?

d  Tybalt is then addressed, and simply. Is this appropriate?

e  His final words are addressed to Juliet. Take each sentence separately and see how it leads to the tragic climax of his suicide.

# Fate and coincidence

1  The tragic end of the *Romeo and Juliet* story is announced in the Prologue by the Chorus. Look up what he says, then search the text of the play for examples of the lovers' sixth sense about their doomed future:

  a **Romeo**   *Act I Scene 4*     *Act II Scene 6*
                       *Act I Scene 5*     *Act V Scene 1*
  b **Juliet**     *Act I Scene 5*     *Act III Scene 2*
                       *Act II Scene 2*   *Act III Scene 5*

What conclusions do you draw about Romeo and Juliet's own awareness of their predicament?

2  The plot of *Romeo and Juliet* contains a number of coincidences.

  a  What is the coincidence about Romeo's two love-affairs?

  b  What is coincidental about the arrival of Paris at the Capulet household?

  c  What is coincidental in connection with the various messages in the play:

    (i) Capulet's as conveyed to his guests by his servant (*Act I Scene 2*)

    (ii) Friar Lawrence's as conveyed by Friar John?

  d  What fatal coincidences occur in the Capulet tomb?

# Contrasts

Complete the following:

    a Romeo's relationship with Mercutio is paralleled by Juliet's to . . .

    b Just as Tybalt is aggressive, . . . is a peacemaker.

    c On the one hand, we have the Capulets. On the other . . .

    d Juliet has a cousin . . . Romeo has a cousin . . .

    e The Prince tries to solve the family feud by law; the Friar tries to solve it by . . .

    f Romeo kills Tybalt and Paris by the sword, but dies by . . .

    g Juliet drugs herself with a potion, but dies by . . .

    h The love of Romeo and Juliet contrasts with the . . . of the Capulets and Montagues.

    i The passion of youth is contrasted with the . . . of old age.

    j Paris woos Juliet according to the rules; Romeo woos Juliet according to his . . .

# Time

1  In *Romeo and Juliet*, time passes very quickly and things
   happen very suddenly. Identify occasions when
   a  love happens at first sight
   b  brawls turn nasty
   c  death is unexpectedly swift
   d  hatred suddenly turns to love
   e  loyalty switches from one person to another
   f  decisions are altered.

2  The action of the play is compressed into the space of about
   four days. Work out a diary of events from the following
   evidence:
   a  Look up *Act III Scene 4*. On the evening of which day is
      Capulet talking to Paris?
   b  From this, deduce what events happened earlier that
      day, and on the previous days.
      (Consult *Act I Scene 1*, *Act I Scene 2*, *Act II Scene 2*, *Act II
      Scene 3*, *Act III Scene 1* and *Act III Scene 3*)
   c  What, therefore, happened on the day following the
      Capulet/Paris discussion?
   d  On what day was the Paris–Juliet marriage finally
      arranged?
   e  Over which night, therefore, did the tomb scene take
      place?

# Examination questions

The following are typical of the kind of examination questions set by the major examining boards:

1 How vividly does Shakespeare capture the effects of hatred and of love in *Romeo and Juliet*? Make close reference to the events of the play and its language.

2 A critic has said that up to the point of Tybalt's death, the play could be thought of as a Romantic Comedy; it is only afterwards that unremitting tragedy is acted out. Would you agree or disagree?

3 'O, I am fortune's fool.' How far is this true of Romeo?

4 'The Friar's decision to marry Romeo and Juliet without the knowledge and consent of their parents is a fatal error of judgement. What happens subsequently is not his fault.' Do you agree?

5 'From forth the fatal loins of these two foes
A pair of star-crossed lovers take their life'
Show how Romeo and Juliet are victims of (a) the society in which they live, (b) malignant fate and (c) their own passions.

6 Estimate the importance of the character of Juliet's Nurse to the success of the play as a whole.

7 At the end of *Romeo and Juliet*, the Prince announces that 'some shall be pardoned, and some punished'. Choose one or more of the survivors, and say how far you think pardon or punishment is deserved.

8 In what ways is Friar Lawrence essential to the plot of *Romeo and Juliet*?

9 'Thou talkest of nothing' says Romeo of Mercutio. What, therefore, is his role in the play? How far was Shakespeare

successful in adding this character to those he found ready-made in his sources?

10 It has been said that Shakespeare's women characters are more mature than their male counterparts. Is this true of *Romeo and Juliet*?

11 'There is so much in *Romeo and Juliet* to disperse the tragic gloom.' Illustrate and discuss such things as humour, romance, excitement and characterisation in the play and say whether these elements have the effect of diminishing its tragic impact.

12 Give an account of the Balcony Scene in which Romeo and Juliet declare their love for each other. What does it reveal of Juliet's character at this stage?

13 Evaluate the poetic and dramatic significance of the soliloquies in *Romeo and Juliet*.

14 Compare Juliet's first appearance with her Mother and the Nurse (*Act I Scene 3*) with her last with them before she drinks the Friar's potion. How much has she changed?

15 We know from the *Prologue* to the play that Romeo and Juliet are doomed. How do you account for the enduring interest of the play?

16 What part do Fate, Chance and Coincidence play in the tragedy of *Romeo and Juliet*?

17 What part does dramatic irony play in the effectiveness of *Romeo and Juliet*?

18 *Romeo and Juliet* contains prose, blank verse, rhyming verse and sonnets. Illustrate the use of each at its most effective, explaining the reasons for your choice.

19 It has been said that, without exception, the characters in *Romeo and Juliet* are stereotypes. How far would you agree?

20 With examples, illustrate the merits and the disadvantages of wordplay in *Romeo and Juliet*.

# One-word-answer quiz

1  Whose name was also the name of a cat in Elizabethan children's stories?

2  What was the name of the Nurse's servant?

3  On what day did Capulet stay up late to tell Paris when the wedding would be?

4  What was the name of the church to be used for the marriage ceremony?

5  What day did Friar Lawrence think was to be the wedding day of Juliet and Paris?

6  On what day did Juliet visit Friar Lawrence and receive a potion?

7  What is 'A madness most discreet, a choking gall, and a preserving sweet' according to Romeo?

8  What was the name of Romeo's servant?

9  What was the name of the Friar sent by Friar Lawrence to Mantua?

10  How many days was Juliet in the tomb before Romeo visited her?

11  On what night of the week did Lady Montague die?

12  Where was the Prince's 'common judgement-place'?

13  What was the name of the Montague servant insulted by Sampson?

14  How many teeth did the Nurse have left?

15  How old was Juliet, according to her father?

16  How old was Lady Capulet, according to the information she gives us?

17  How many years did Capulet first think should pass before Juliet should marry?

18  What, according to Romeo, was the name gaolers gave to the merry spirits of condemned men?

19  Under what kind of tree did Benvolio see Romeo on his early-morning walk?

20  At what time in the morning did Benvolio question Romeo about his sadness?

21  At what time in the morning was Juliet to contact Romeo after the Masque?

22  At what time did the Nurse return from her first visit to Romeo?

23  How many hours was she away?

24  How many times had the Capulets and Montagues disturbed the peace, according to the Prince?

25  At what time in the morning was the Nurse sent to fetch spices?

26  What was Cupid's physical handicap?

27  Under what kind of tree did Paris order his Page to lie in the churchyard?

28  How many tools did Romeo have in order to break into the Capulet vault?

29  What did he say he was intending to recover from the tomb?

30  What 'by any other word would smell as sweet'?

31  Which order of Friars did Friar Lawrence belong to?

32  What tune did Peter request the musicians to play?

33  Who, according to the Nurse, was 'a man of wax'?

34  Where did Romeo take up residence after his banishment?

35  Approximately how long was Romeo in the vault before Friar Lawrence arrived?

36  What was hanging from the ceiling of the apothecary's shop in Mantua?

37  How many ducats did Romeo pay for the poison he bought?

38  What was the penalty for selling poison in Mantua?

39  What was Rosaline's relationship to Capulet?

40  What was the relationship between Signor Valentio and Tybalt?

41  What herb was used as a symbol of remembrance at weddings and funerals?

42  How many children did the Capulets have?

43  How many cooks were to be hired to prepare the Capulet's wedding-feast?

44  Of what material were the statues of Romeo and Juliet to be made to commemorate their lives?

45  What caused the Capulet's dove-house to shake when Juliet was a toddler?

46  What drink did the Nurse call out for on discovering Juliet, apparently dead?

47  Who 'plaits the manes of horses in the night'?

48  On what tree did Juliet say the nightingale sang in her garden?

49  What was the name of the Nurse's daughter?

50  What was the name of Mercutio's brother?

# What's missing?

Complete the following quotations:

1 The pretty fool, it stinted, and said ' . . .'

2 We'll have no Cupid hoodwinked with a scarf, / Bearing . . . painted bow of lath.

3 He jests at scars that . . .

4 O, I have bought the mansion of a love, / But . . .

5 Never was a story of more woe / Than . . .

6 Therefore we'll have . . . / And there an end

7 Death, that hath ta'en her hence to make me wail . . .

8 O, in this love you love your child so ill / That . . .

9 O, then I see . . . hath been with you

10 Marry, sir, 'tis an ill cook . . .

11 O Fortune, Fortune! All men . . .

12 Happiness courts thee in her best array, / But . . .

13 Farewell – God knows when . . .

14 But soft! What light through yonder window breaks? / It . . .

15 Ah me! How sweet is love itself possessed / When . . .

16 O serpent heart, hid with a flowering face! / Did . . .

17 Death, that hath sucked the honey of thy breath, / Hath . . .

18 O mischief, thou art swift / To . . .

19 It was the nightingale, and not . . . / That pierced the fearful hollow of thine ear.

20 Stay not, be gone; live and hereafter say . . .

21 O, thou untaught! What manners is in this, / To . . .

22 Death lies upon her, like an untimely frost upon . . .

23 Alack, my child is dead, And . . .

24 If love be blind, love . . .

25 That 'banished', that one word 'banished', / Hath . . .

26 Though fond nature bids us all lament, / Yet . . .

27 Her chariot is an empty hazel-nut, made by . . .

28 Alas, that love, so gentle in his view, / Should be so . . .

29 Show me a mistress who is passing fair! / What doth her Beauty serve . . .?

30 This bud of love . . . may prove a beauteous flower when next we meet

31 Parting is such sweet sorrow, That . . .

32 Now by Saint Peter's Church and Peter too, / He . . .

33 Love is a smoke, made with . . . sighs

34 Tut, man, one fire burns out another's burning . . .

35 It seems she hangs upon the cheek of night . . . ear

36 The earth that's natures mother is her tomb; / What . . .

37 But passion lends them power . . . sweet

38 What's in a name? . . . as sweet

39 Love goes toward love as . . . / But love from love . . .

40 No, 'tis not so deep as a well, nor so wide as a church door but . . .

41 Oh, she is rich in beauty; only poor / That . . .

42 Young men's love then lies / Not . . . but . . .

43 He that is strucken blind cannot forget . . .

44 How silver-sweet sound lovers' tongues by night, / Like . . .

45 True, I talk of dreams which are . . . brain

46 Oh, that I were a glove . . .!

47 O, he's a lovely gentleman! Romeo's a . . . to him

48 Here's much to do with hate, but . . .

49 Out, you green-sickness carrion! Out . . . You . . .!

50 If I profane . . . this holy shrine

## More plays in the
## SHAKESPEARE MADE EASY
## series

All these plays are available from your bookshop or newsagent or you can order them direct. Just tick the titles you want and complete the order form below.

| | | |
|---|---|---|
| —— | MACBETH | £1.95 |
| —— | ROMEO AND JULIET | £1.95 |
| —— | THE MERCHANT OF VENICE | £1.95 |
| —— | JULIUS CAESAR | £1.95 |

*Available Autumn 1984*

| | | |
|---|---|---|
| —— | HENRY IV PART ONE | £1.95 |
| —— | A MIDSUMMER NIGHT'S DREAM | £1.95 |

ARROW BOOKS, BOOKSERVICE BY POST, PO BOX 29, DOUGLAS, ISLE OF MAN, BRITISH ISLES

Please enclose a cheque or postal order made out to Arrow Books Limited for the amount due including 10p per book for postage and packing for orders within the UK.

*Please print clearly*

Name _____

Address _____

_____

Whilst every effort is made to keep prices down and to keep popular books in print, Arrow Books cannot guarantee that prices will be the same as those advertised here or that the books will be available.
This applies to orders from the UK only. Overseas customers should order direct from:
The Export Dept, Hutchinson House, 17/21 Conway Street, London W1P 6JD, UK.